Police Investigative Interviews and Interpreting

Context, Challenges, and Strategies

Advances in Police Theory and Practice Series

Series Editor: Dilip K. Das

**Police Investigative Interviews and Interpreting:
Context, Challenges, and Strategies**
Sedat Mulayim, Miranda Lai, and Caroline Norma

Crime Linkage: Theory, Research, and Practice
Jessica Woodhams and Craig Bennell

Policing White Collar Crime: Characteristics of White Collar Criminals
Petter Gottschalk

Honor-Based Violence: Policing and Prevention
Karl Anton Roberts, Gerry Campbell, and Glen Lloyd

Policing and the Mentally Ill: International Perspectives
Duncan Chappell

Security Governance, Policing, and Local Capacity
Jan Froestad with Clifford D. Shearing

Policing in Hong Kong: History and Reform
Kam C. Wong

Police Performance Appraisals: A Comparative Perspective
Serdar Kenan Gul and Paul O'Connell

Los Angeles Police Department Meltdown: The Fall of the Professional-Reform Model of Policing
James Lasley

Financial Crimes: A Global Threat
Maximillian Edelbacher, Peter Kratcoski, and Michael Theil

Police Integrity Management in Australia: Global Lessons for Combating Police Misconduct
Louise Porter and Tim Prenzler

The Crime Numbers Game: Management by Manipulation
John A. Eterno and Eli B. Silverman

The International Trafficking of Human Organs: A Multidisciplinary Perspective
Leonard Territo and Rande Matteson

Police Reform in China
Kam C. Wong

Mission-Based Policing
John P. Crank, Dawn M. Irlbeck, Rebecca K. Murray, and Mark Sundermeier

The New Khaki: The Evolving Nature of Policing in India
Arvind Verma

Cold Cases: An Evaluation Model with Follow-up Strategies for Investigators
James M. Adcock and Sarah L. Stein

Policing Organized Crime: Intelligence Strategy Implementation
Petter Gottschalk

Security in Post-Conflict Africa: The Role of Nonstate Policing
Bruce Baker

Community Policing and Peacekeeping
Peter Grabosky

Community Policing: International Patterns and Comparative Perspectives
Dominique Wisler and Ihekwoaba D. Onwudiwe

Police Corruption: Preventing Misconduct and Maintaining Integrity
Tim Prenzler

FORTHCOMING

Cold Cases: Evaluation Models with Follow-up Strategies for Investigators,
Second Edition
James M. Adcock and Sarah L. Stein

Democratic Policing
Darren Palmer

Corruption, Fraud, Organized Crime, and the Shadow Economy
Maximilian Edelbacher, Peter C. Kratcoski, and Bojan Dobovsek

Policing Terrorism: Research Studies into
Police Counter-terrorism Investigations
David Lowe

Collaborative Policing: Police, Academics, Professionals, and Communities
Working Together for Education, Training, and Program Implementation
Peter C. Kratcoski and Maximilian Edelbacher

Islamic Women in Policing: A Contradiction in Terms?
Tonita Murray

Female Criminals: An Examination and Interpretation of Female Offending
Venessa Garcia

Police Investigative Interviews and Interpreting

Context, Challenges, and Strategies

Sedat Mulayim

Miranda Lai   Caroline Norma

CRC Press
Taylor & Francis Group
Boca Raton London New York

CRC Press is an imprint of the
Taylor & Francis Group, an **informa** business

CRC Press
Taylor & Francis Group
6000 Broken Sound Parkway NW, Suite 300
Boca Raton, FL 33487-2742

First issued in paperback 2019

ISBN-13: 978-1-4822-4255-3 (hbk)
ISBN-13: 978-0-367-87012-6 (pbk)

Library of Congress Cataloging-in-Publication Data

Mulayim, Sedat.
   Police investigative interviews and interpreting : context, challenges, and strategies / Sedat Mulayim, Miranda Lai, Caroline Norma.
      pages cm -- (Advances in police theory and practice ; 22)
   Includes bibliographical references and index.
   ISBN 978-1-4822-4255-3 (hardback)
   1. Interviewing in law enforcement. 2. Public service interpreting. 3. Translating and interpreting. I. Title.

HV8073.3.M85 2015
363.25'4--dc23   2014011867

Visit the Taylor & Francis Web site at
http://www.taylorandfrancis.com

and the CRC Press Web site at
http://www.crcpress.com

We dedicate this book to all those practicing interpreters who provide a critical, albeit often under acknowledged, service within the context of law enforcement and criminal justice administration, thus assisting in implementing the principles of natural justice and procedural fairness.

Contents

Foreword

Police forces are set up to enforce criminal law and protect the public from crime. Interaction with the police is often initiated because an offense may have been committed affecting one or more members of the public either as suspects or witnesses. Often an interview will need to be conducted to elicit further information and add to the evidence. Police interviews can be daunting, if not intimidating, for most members of the public, not so much because of the uniforms, concrete buildings, and fluorescent lighting, as the strict formal procedures and highly unusual discourse. The interaction process is further complicated when the suspect or witness does not speak the language in which the interview is conducted. This is where professional interpreters may be required.

There are a substantial number of publications that cover broader cross-cultural communication issues and the role of interpreters in court settings. However, the police interview stage in the criminal justice process has received much less attention. This book (*Police Investigative Interviews and Interpreting: Context, Challenges, and Strategies*) is the first attempt, to my knowledge, that has examined in detail the dynamics of how interpreters work in police interviews, especially within the current major investigative interviewing paradigms, and it fills a significant gap. The book can be a great resource for professional interpreters and law enforcement officers who work with interpreters in investigative interviews.

Although the subject matter of this book is limited to police interview settings, the underlying rationale for how interpreters should be working applies to other professional areas that rely on interviews to collect information. I hope this valuable resource will lead to greater interest by researchers and academics in this highly specialized field. I congratulate the authors on this worthy endeavor.

Dr. Barry Turner, Adjunct Professor
RMIT University
Senior interpreter educator/trainer, examiner, and practitioner
Melbourne, Australia

Series Editor's Preface

While the literature on police and allied subjects is growing exponentially, its impact upon day-to-day policing remains limited. The two worlds of research and practice in relation to policing remain disconnected, even though cooperation between the two is growing. A major reason for this is that the two groups speak different languages. The research work is published in hard-to-access journals and presented in a manner that is difficult to comprehend. On the other hand, police practitioners tend not to mix with researchers and remain secretive about their work. Consequently, there is little dialogue between the two and almost no attempt to learn from one another. Dialogue across the globe, amongst researchers and practitioners situated in different continents, is, of course, even more limited.

I attempted to address this problem by starting the International Police Executive Symposium (IPES) (www.ipes.info) where a common platform has brought the two together. IPES is now in its 17th year. The annual meetings that constitute most major annual events of the organization have been hosted in all parts of the world. Several publications have come out of these deliberations and a new collaborative community of scholars and police officers has been created whose membership runs into several hundreds.

Another attempt was to begin a new journal, aptly called *Police Practice and Research: An International Journal* (*PPR*), which has opened the gate to practitioners to share their work and experiences. The journal has attempted to focus upon issues that help bring the two onto a single platform. *PPR* completed its 15th year in 2014. It is certainly evidence of growing collaboration between police research and practice that *PPR*, which began with four issues a year, expanded into five issues in its 4th year and, now, is issued six times a year.

Clearly, these attempts, despite their successes, remain limited. Conferences and journal publications do help create a body of knowledge and an association of police activists, but cannot address substantial issues in depth. The limitations of time and space preclude larger discussions and more authoritative expositions that can provide stronger and broader linkages between the two worlds.

It is this realization of the increasing dialogue between police research and practice that has encouraged many of us—my close colleagues and I connected closely with IPES and *PPR* across the world—to conceive and implement a new attempt in this direction. I am now embarking on a book series, Advances in Police Theory and Practice, that seeks to attract writers from all parts of the world. Further, the attempt is to find practitioner contributors. The objective is to make the series a serious contribution to our knowledge of policing as well as to improve police practices. The focus is not only on work that describes the best and most successful police practices, but also work that challenges current paradigms and breaks new ground to prepare police for the 21st century. The series forges comparative analyses that highlight achievements in distant parts of the world as well as comparisons that encourage in-depth examination of specific problems confronting a particular police force.

An increasingly globalized world has meant members of police forces around the globe find themselves having to deal with suspects and witnesses who are separated by a language barrier more often now than at any time in history. This is becoming a serious issue in all aspects of policing, from community policing to major international crime investigations. Most critically difficult are investigative interviews involving suspects and witnesses who speak another language. Investigating officers often have to rely on a third party, often an interpreter, to assist with communication. This book deals with how this communication can be enhanced by introducing readers to the subtleties of interlingual communication and the profession of interpreting in the context of major investigative interviewing paradigms. It provides a practical discussion of how interpreting can best be used by police officers to achieve their aims, and highlights areas where these aims can be compromised due to interpreting issues.

It is a comprehensively researched and practically written resource, which, I believe, will be of benefit to members of police forces and other law enforcement agencies around the world and interpreters who intend to specialize in this significant field.

It is hoped that through this series it will be possible to accelerate the process of building knowledge about policing and help bridge the gap between the two worlds—the world of police research and police practice. This is an invitation to police scholars and practitioners across the world to come and join in this venture.

Dilip K. Das, Series Editor

Founding president, International Police
Executive Symposium
http://www.ipes.info
Series editor, Advances in Police Theory and
Practice

(CRC Press/Taylor & Francis Group)
Series editor, Interviews with Global Leaders in Police, Courts, and Prisons
(CRC Press/Taylor & Francis Group)
Series editor, PPR Special Issues as Books
(Routledge/Taylor & Francis Group)
Founding editor-in-chief, Police Practice and Research: An
International Journal
(Routledge/Taylor & Francis Group)
http://www.tandfonline.com/GPPR

Prologue

No two languages are ever sufficiently similar to be considered as representing the same social reality. The worlds in which different societies live are distinct worlds, not merely the same world with different labels attached.

Edward Sapir (1956, p. 69)

Professional interpreting and translating always takes place within another professional activity, such as diplomacy, conferences, business meetings, and public service delivery. In their capacities as interpreters and translators with extensive experience and through their academic research in this field, the authors have seen an increasing need to look at interpreters and translators within the highly specialized professional activity of investigative interviewing. They believe this is best done through an interdisciplinary approach. They see an unmet need for interpreters who are well informed of the dynamics of investigative interviewing and have skills and knowledge to deal with the complexities of transferring language across linguistic and cultural divides, and, at the same time, remain faithful to the intentions and strategies used by the interviewing officers. They also believe an understanding of how interpreters work will better equip interviewing officers to control their interviews effectively, even though the communication is being done via a third party.

The authors have made every effort to use plain English alongside professional terms to facilitate understanding by a wider audience. The issues covered in this book are not intended to be culture- or language-specific. Examples provided illustrate areas of concern commonly encountered across a wide of range of languages in court interpreting as well as police interview settings.

Sedat Mulayim
Miranda Lai
Caroline Norma

About the Authors

Sedat Mulayim is the current discipline head of translating and interpreting programs at RMIT (Royal Melbourne Institute of Technology) University in Melbourne, Australia. He has a Master of Arts (translation studies) by research degree and is currently undertaking his PhD research in public service translation and interpreting. He has developed and delivered training programs for interpreters in legal and police settings in Australia and overseas. He also has produced resources for other professionals on how to work with interpreters.

He is a certified interpreter and translator in the Turkish language and has over 20 years of experience in interpreting in police interviews and courts. His research interests include police interpreting, professional ethics global security issues in multilingual settings, and public service translation and interpreting.

Miranda Lai is currently a lecturer and trainer in interpreting and translating at RMIT University in Melbourne, Australia. She is undertaking her PhD research into PEACE (preparation and planning, engage and explain, account, closure, and evaluate) police interviewing mediated by interpreters. She has developed and delivered training programs for interpreters in Australia and overseas. She is a certified interpreter and translator in the Chinese language and has many years of practice experience. Her research interests include investigative interviewing in multilingual settings and public service translation and interpreting.

Caroline Norma, PhD, is a lecturer in the Master of Translation Studies degree at RMIT University in Melbourne, Australia. She is a certified Japanese translator, and conducts research in the area of feminist approaches to translating and interpreting. She has worked with Victoria Police in researching sexual assault reporting.

Acknowledgments

The authors would like to express their gratitude to Professor Dilip K. Das for the inspiration and vision he has provided. Professor Das is a strong advocate of cross-fertilization of police research and practice. Also, his guidance to the authors on accessible language for the broader audience of law enforcement and interpreting practitioners has been invaluable. The authors would also like to thank Adjunct Professor Barry Turner, former head of the Translating and Interpreting Program at RMIT University, for his ongoing support and encouragement.

Finally, Ms. Mavis Clifford deserves our thanks for her help with the arduous and frightening task of proofreading the manuscript a number of times.

Introduction

Good clear communication between people is a fundamental feature of a functional society. When a society becomes multi-lingual, and, therefore, multicultural, the task of maintaining that good clear communication becomes more difficult. A lack of communication can and does lead to social breakdown. It falls to the availability of good-quality interpreting to create a bridge between the different language and cultural groups within a community. It is essential, therefore, that interpreters are well trained, experienced, and fluent in both languages and have a clear understanding of the cultures of both parties in any interpreting event.

Interpreters are needed in everyday as well as extraordinary situations. The Seal Team 6 that carried out the raid on Osama Bin Laden's compound in Pakistan in May 2011 included an interpreter. The French sailor who was rescued in January 2013 from his stricken yacht off the Australian coast required the services of an interpreter in order to communicate with the rescue team. A Melbourne student pilot who performed an emergency landing after circling the skies for 3 hours was assisted (from the ground) by instructors via an interpreter. Many international organizations and agencies conduct their meetings, conferences, and events in multiple languages with the assistance of interpreters.

Equally, and as importantly, local hospitals, social welfare offices, and schools in multilingual countries require interpreters on a daily basis in communicating with patients, clients, and parents who may not be proficient in the official language. Interpreters may even assist in ceremonies and social events, such as political speeches, weddings, or funerals. In short, any human activity may involve an interpreter if the parties in these activities do not share a common language and they have a need to communicate.

Interpreting, therefore, is broadly defined as the act of transferring meaning *orally* between two languages for the benefit of parties who do not share a common language. In this broader sense, interpreting may be provided by family members, friends, or by bilingual staff members; for example, social workers, counselors, or community liaison officers. This book, however, is concerned with the *professional* activity of interpreting.

Crucial elements differentiate professional interpreting from ad hoc interpreting. Firstly, professional interpreters are engaged in situations that require impartiality, highly specialized linguistic skills, and cultural knowledge. Secondly, professional interpreters are needed in a range of business and administrative activities. Interpreters help clients, for example, to access public services, such as housing or income support, or help patients during medical consultations. Interpreters also are required to provide services during police interviews as well as at hearings in a court of law or a tribunal. Finally, and perhaps most importantly, professional interpreting is one of the few professions conducted wholly within another professional activity. This last distinguishing characteristic of professional interpreting has significant implications for the decisions professional interpreters make. Interpreters are bound to respect the objectives and intentions of the speakers (i.e., they should not sanitize or embellish communication) and, primarily, to respect the rules and ethics of the institutions in which they are working. The nature of such activities, and of law enforcement in particular, requires an impartial and highly competent person to enable communication.

The Specialization of Interpreting

Interpreting has become a more specialized profession precisely because of the increase in the complexity of the professions within which interpreters function.

A quick scan of interpreter and translator certification around the world shows that the main areas of specialization are conference interpreting (e.g., for the United Nations and European Parliament meetings), public service interpreting, health interpreting, and legal interpreting. One should note, however, that there is no consensus on the boundaries of where one type of interpreting ends and where the other starts. For example, an international conference on HIV/AIDS requires interpreters who are specialized in both conference interpreting and health interpreting.

The domain of legal interpreting is also subject to debate. Some scholars argue that legal interpreting covers any interpreting of a legal nature—in courts, lawyer consultations, police interviews—while others narrow the term to exclude anything outside of court settings. The authors of this book agree with the positions taken by Virginia Benmaman (1997) and Sandra Hale (2007)* that legal interpreting includes the full spectrum of the justice system, from interviews with law enforcement officers to lawyer–client conferences and court and tribunal hearings.

Police Interpreting

Within the broader field of legal interpreting, police interpreting is emerging as a highly specialized, distinct application of interpreting.

---

* Benmaman notes that the term *legal interpreting* is used interchangeably with *court interpreting* and *judiciary interpreting*, and argues that court interpreting (synonymous with judiciary interpreting) "is but one form of legal interpreting, which shares many common characteristics with other types of legal interpreting" (Benmaman, 1997, p. 180–181). In the same vein, Hale explains that "these domains share the underlying legal system they serve, legal concepts and some of their discourses. However, each domain differs in terms of the relationship between interlocutors, the goal of the interaction, the privacy and the formality of the event, the roles of the participants, the role of language, and, as a consequence, the implications for interpreters" (Hale, 2007, p. 65).

Police interpreting mainly takes place in police–suspect interviews and in obtaining statements from witnesses and victims. Interpreting is increasingly required in multilingual communities as members of ethnic communities come in contact with law enforcement agencies. Furthermore, since September 11, 2001, security has become a global issue beyond national or regional borders, and this has resulted in an increase in the employment of qualified and trained interpreters by law enforcement agencies in the investigation- and intelligence-gathering stages of their operations. Many investigations involve interpreters for the duration of the operation, from the surveillance stages to arrest and interviews.

The single most important element in police interpreting is that all utterances produced immediately may be presented later to a court as evidence. While in all other settings, interpreting is for the benefit of the parties who are present in the conversation, either face-to-face or via communication media, all utterances exchanged between police and interviewees (suspects and/or witnesses) are knowingly "produced for a third party" (Heritage, 1985; Greatbatch, 1988), "produced to be overheard" (Heydon, 2005, p. 39), or produced "for a future audience" (Cotterill, 2002, p. 124).

Keeping in mind the "future audience," i.e., the court, police interviews must follow highly prescriptive patterns: a recording preamble to identify date, time, and participating parties; the police caution to (in Australia, similar to the Miranda warning in the United States); the actual interview; and the *final* statement confirming the time of the conclusion of the interview. In addition, the police need to follow strict guidelines about how they say or explain things. The procedures highlight the power asymmetry, i.e., the unequal power relations, between the interviewer and the interviewee inherent in police interviews. While issues of power may arise in other interpreting settings (e.g., in education, health, or social welfare), power asymmetry is much more visible in police interviews. It is manifested in the allocation of questions asked exclusively by the interviewing officer, while the interviewee must respond. Furthermore, the interviewing officer not only initiates the questions, but also controls the topics of the interview. Any deviations from the topics or line of enquiry are "characteristically repaired" (Heydon, 2005, p. 100). In other words, the police officer will steer the interviewee back to the topic under discussion. These features—utterances being produced for a third party, prescribed language and sequence, and power asymmetry—make police interviews not just a different type of interpreting, but a distinct genre of institutional discourse.

Significance of Interpreting in the Investigative Stage of Criminal Justice

In most countries, the criminal justice process broadly involves three main stages: investigative (police), adjudicative (courts), and correctional (prisons and other correctional programs). Police interviews, being an "upstream event" (Cotterill, 2002, p. 111), are often conducted long before a case goes to trial. In response to questions by the investigating police officers, suspects or witnesses often make statements possibly incriminating themselves in the case under investigation, particularly if they have difficulty with communication in a language that is not their mother tongue. Susan Berk-Seligson, a U.S. linguistics professor, (2009, p. 2) argues that understanding the language of those who command the language of the institution, and the ability to express oneself fully in the interaction, are central to the due process of justice. Legal academics Laster and Taylor (1994, p. 136) thus argue that "access to an interpreter during police questioning is probably more significant than the right to an interpreter in court proceedings."

In police interviews, suspects or witnesses are often more vulnerable to the fallout of poor communication whenever they have limited or no opportunities to seek advice or assistance from other professionals, including lawyers, counselors, advocates, and family and friends. Lack of interpreting services or poor interpreting at the police station may come back "to haunt [suspects and/or witnesses] at subsequent stages of the judicial process" (Berk-Seligson, 2009, p. 215). In countries like Australia and the United Kingdom, police will arrange for a professional interpreter for suspects or witnesses who are judged to lack sufficient English language skills to be interviewed. Unlike in the United States, where bilingual police officers are still seen to conduct interviews in Spanish and act as interpreters (Berk-Seligson, 2009), in Australia and the United Kingdom, even if a police officer or legal representative of a suspect is bilingual and is able to interpret, a publicly funded independent interpreter must be provided for reasons of objectivity and impartiality.

To date, the field of police interpreting has received limited attention in the literature. Most of the research conducted into legal interpreting has concentrated on the courtroom setting (Hale, 2007, pp. 79, 90). In the comparatively small corpus on police interpreting, various scholars have explored a range of topics. Linguist and interpreting academic Dr. Alexander Krouglov (1999) analyzes police interpreting as an example of how interpreters deal with colloquialisms and hedges (words or phrases to mitigate the power of a statement), as well as forms of address and other forms of politeness. He argues strongly that interpreters should preserve the interviewee's style and register, otherwise it may lead to "inaccurate social or psychological evaluations" of the interviewee (p. 295) (also Hale, 2007, p. 74–75). This view is consistent with the research outcomes from the field of court interpreting. On the inherently challenging nature of police interpreting, practitioner and educator Ester S. M. Leung (2003) points out the issues arising from police interpreting assignments (in the United Kingdom) where interpreters are given short notice, have a lack of prior information about the topic of the assignment, and have to face dialect issues in some languages that only become apparent when the interpreter arrives at the police station. These seemingly peripheral aspects of police interpreting, in fact, significantly impinge upon the best possible interpreting quality expected by the interviewing police officers.

In Chapter 3 of this book, the authors specifically tackle the challenges of police interpreting arising out of the interpreter's professional role boundaries, including issues of conduct as well as language issues of both a linguistic and nonlinguistic nature.

Best Interpreting Outcome and Interviewer Competency

As explained previously, interpreters in Australia are publicly funded for reasons of objectivity and impartiality, which means professional interpreters must have in mind to serve both conversing clients equally. In the interest of achieving the best police interview outcomes for all parties involved, Perez and Wilson (2007) advocate that, instead of relying solely on the competency of the interpreter, police officers should work with interpreters, thus highlighting the significance of cooperation between the two professions for successful communication. Two further studies come to the same conclusion. Swedish interpreting studies professor, Cecelia Wadensjö, asserts that, in interpreter-mediated interactions in any setting, "the meaning conveyed in and by talk is partly a joint product [of all participants]" (Wadensjö, 1998, p. 8). Cynthia Roy, a professor in sign language interpreting, also regards the interpreter as not solely responsible for either the success or failure of interpreted interaction, and believes that "all three participants [the professional, the client, and the interpreter] jointly produce this event, and all three are responsible..."(Roy, 2000, p. 63).

The competence of interviewers in the criminal justice context is recognized in literature. U.S. criminologists Lord and Cowan (2011) acknowledge that the interviewers are "expected to communicate with people from a variety of cultures and languages, often using translators." Their subsequent suggestion only serves to highlight the complexity and difficulty of the interpreter's task:

> ... the only genuine means of developing a deep understanding of any culture is through visiting the other countries, learning another country's language, and attempting first hand to assimilate into a different culture (p. 168).

Lord and Cowen stop short of elaborating how police investigators can collaborate with professional interpreters to achieve the best possible interview outcomes, which, in the opinion of the authors, would have been more useful. Instead, they suggest that police investigators acquire foreign languages to overcome culture and language barriers. As professions become more field-specific and technically specialized in their own right, leaving cross-cultural and cross-lingual communication to someone other than an independent professional interpreter, in the authors' opinion, is a proposition that calls for further debate. The authors' position is supported by Berk-Seligson (2000; 2009) who has found issues of compromised neutrality when U.S. police use bilingual officers as interpreters in interrogations.

Interpreter Competency

When things go wrong in an interpreter-mediated communicative event, interpreters are often the first to be suspected of causing the miscommunication. Indeed, the quality of interpreters' work is sometimes called into question. The range of issues raised about the quality of interpreting include linguistic aspects, such as the use of an incorrect equivalent for a word or expression, and nonlinguistic aspects, such as the interpreter asking questions, omitting details, or giving advice to the parties involved.

Linguistics researcher Ikuko Nakane (2009), in her analysis of two drug importation cases by Japanese nationals to Australia, demonstrates how interpreters sometimes deviate from a faithful sound box role by, for example, editing the interviewee's answer (in order to respond better to the questions put to them by the interviewing officer) or answering a question on behalf of the interviewee (without interpreting the question, using the information they obtained so far in the interview). Nakane asserts that interpreters do so because of their desire to maintain a competent image or out of a misguided preference to maintain the relevance of the question and answer sequence. She argues that interpreters making such role shifts from a "faithful sound box" to a participating conversing party in police interviews may not be warranted and may be in breach of their code of ethics.

A classic illustration of how things can go wrong when the competency of the interpreter is brought into question is the 1992 case against a group of Japanese nationals arrested at the Melbourne Airport and charged with the importation of heroin for commercial purposes. This case is documented in *Katsuno et al. 2006 v. Australia* (2006).* Further discussions about this case appear in Chapter 1 of this book. Members of the group were convicted, but an appeal in 1995 to the Supreme Court of Victoria listed eight areas of interpreter incompetence to support their appeal. In response to the claims of interpreting errors raised by the members of the group, the Victorian government claimed that the standards of interpreting expected by the defendants was unattainably high, given nuances in translation that will inevitably occur in the rendition of one language into another. The standard of interpreting provided to the defendants conformed with the standards set out by the European Convention on Human Rights (ECHR) in *Kamasinski v. Austria* (1989); therefore, the Victorian

---

* Refer to the following link for the case details from the United Nations Human Rights Committee. http://www.ag.gov.au/RightsAndProtections/HumanRights/ DisabilityStandards/Documents/KatsunoOrsvAustralia-Viewsof31102006.doc

government claimed the errors were not significant enough to change the outcome of the case.

The defendants took their case to the UN Human Rights Committee in 2006, relying upon Article 6(3)(e) of the European Convention on Human Rights, which stipulates a suspect's right, not only to an interpreter, but also to good-quality, competent interpreting:[*]

> Defendants have the right to free assistance of an interpreter under Article 6(3)(e). That assistance relates to both oral statements made at the trial and to documents pertaining to the dispute. A defendant should have enough evidence to allow him to defend himself and/or protect his interests during adjudication. The obligation of the competent authorities is not limited to the appointment of an interpreter but extends to judgment over the competence of a specific interpreter (UN CCPR, 2006).

The right to quality interpreting is endorsed by interpreting practitioner and academic Ruth Morris (2008, p. 34):

> Along a continuum of interlingual interpreting, which begins with police investigations and may end in a Supreme Court, consistent quality must be assured in order to comply with the standards of justice to which enlightened countries aspire and lay claim.

While governments in countries like Australia have expended a great deal of legislative and policy effort over the past 3 decades in bolstering access to interpreting services in the courts by migrants, indigenous people, and deaf members of the community, very little attention has been directed to improvements to those services in other stages of the criminal justice system. The "standards of justice" that Morris refers to should be established not just in the downstream court system, but also well before this in the upstream criminal justice

---

[*] If readers are interested in more case studies of the provision of interpreting service, or otherwise, the following cases from the European Court of Human Rights should be of interest:

Luedicke, Belkacem and Koc v. Germany, 1978
Kamasinski v. Austria, No. 9783/82, 1989
Mutatis mutandis Artico v. Italy, No. 6694/74, 1980.
Cuscani v. UK, no. 32771/96
Brozicek v. Italy, 1989

process, which involves agencies like the police and community legal centers.

The Right to Access an Interpreter

The rights to liberty and security, and to a fair trial, are fundamental human rights protected by the European Convention on Human Rights (ECHR). They include the right to interpretation where needed. To anyone who is arrested or charged with a criminal offence, Articles 5 and 6 of the ECHR, respectively cover the right of the individual to "be informed promptly, *in a language which he understands*," (italics added) of either "the reasons for his arrest and of any charge against him" or "the nature and cause of the accusation against him." Article 6 even goes so far as to say that the person charged with a criminal offense has the right to "*have the free assistance of an interpreter* if he cannot understand or speak the language used in the court" (italics added).

Similarly, the United Nations' International Covenant—Civil and Political Rights, Article 14 (3) states:

> In the determination of any criminal charge against him, everyone shall be entitled to the following minimum guarantees, in full equality:
>
> (a) To be informed promptly and in detail *in a language which he understands* of the nature and cause of the charge against him …
>
> (f) To have the *free assistance of an interpreter* if he cannot understand or speak the language used in court …

(Italics added) (UN, 1966)

How have these UN recommendations been implemented in national jurisdictions? The English and Welsh police forces are obliged to provide interpreting services under the Police and Criminal Evidence (PACE) Act 1984 Section 13, Code C: Detention, Treatment and Questioning of Persons (PACE, 1984).

In the United States, the provision of interpreting services in the federal jurisdiction is well regulated under the Court Interpreters Act of 1978 (Benmaman, 1992); however, "current state, county, and municipal practice are still unclear. Constitutional provision for the right to an interpreter exists in two states only: California and New

Mexico" (p. 446). The problem of police failing to use interpreters at all in their work is discussed by Katrina Miller (2001) in an article that empirically found in relation to deaf suspects in the United States that:

> ... by far the most commonly attempted method of communication used by law enforcement was spoken English (i.e., no accommodation at all), which was used during 40.9% of the arrests. Court records indicate that 22.7% of suspects in these cases had to communicate through signing family members, friends, or law enforcement employees; 13.6% of the suspects were provided with professional interpreters at the time of arrest or during subsequent legal proceedings (p. 329).

At the state level in the United States, the use of competent impartial interpreters does not seem to be as clearly mandated as is the case in the United Kingdom, and indeed in Australia. Linguistics professor Susan Berk-Seligson (2009) writes about documented cases in the United States in which the use of bilingual police officers and unqualified interpreters led to confessions that were proved later to have resulted from lack of access to impartial and competent interpreters. She recommends the discontinuation of the use of bilingual police officers and the provision of professional interpreters in police interviews (p. 215). Although the underprovision of interpreting services across every spectrum of public service is still a big issue in the United States, some leadership has come from the federal level in an attempt to rectify the situation. For example, the United States Executive Order 13166 "Improving Access to Services for Persons with Limited English Proficiency" (2000) dictates that "... the Federal Government [should] provide ... and fund ... an array of services that can be made accessible to otherwise eligible persons who are not proficient in the English language" (U.S. Department of Justice, 2012).

In Australia, the right to have an independent qualified interpreter has been legislated at both the federal and state levels. The Commonwealth Crimes Act 1914 states that any interview conducted under its jurisdiction cannot commence until an interpreter is present: "the official must, before starting to question the person, arrange for the presence of an interpreter and defer the questioning or investigation until the interpreter is present" (Laster & Taylor, 1994, p. 137; Hale, 2007, p. 69). The Crimes Act 1958 (Victoria) Section 464D stipulates the following right to an interpreter in its state criminal jurisdiction:

(1) If a person in custody does not have a knowledge of the English language that is sufficient to enable the person to understand the questioning, an investigating official must, before any questioning or investigation under section 464A(2) commences, arrange for the presence of a competent interpreter and defer the questioning or investigation until the interpreter is present AUSTLII 2013(a).

In the state of New South Wales, Evidence Act 1995 (NSW) Section 30 AUSTLII 2013(b) gives statutory recognition to the right of a witness to give evidence through an interpreter:

A witness may give evidence about a fact through an interpreter unless the witness can understand and speak the English language sufficiently to enable the witness to understand, and to make an adequate reply to, questions that may be put about the fact.

It is worth noting, though, that these two states only fund interpreting services for criminal proceedings, but not civil ones.

Furthermore, when it comes to police operations in Australia, using interpreters has become standard, thus mandated in their "Standing Orders" (Hale, 2007, p. 69; Ozolins, 2009, p. 23). And police "have come to the understanding that it is in their interests to employ the services of an interpreter" (Hale, 2007, p. 69) in order to protect the admissibility in court of the evidence they obtained from persons they interviewed.

Summary

As the world becomes more globalized and societies more multicultural due to the growing mobility of people, interpreter-assisted communication will play an increasingly crucial role in human interactions. Governments that have to deal with multilingualism when providing public services to their residents are increasingly moving to offering interpreting services in order to fulfill their duty of care and the requirement of respecting human rights. Precisely out of these concerns is an independent professional interpreting service provided to enable people who do not speak the language of the court to not only be physically present, but also have complete "linguistic presence" (de Jongh, 2012, p. 4) in the courtroom. In the same spirit, the authors argue that when members of the public are being interviewed by the police—the "upstream event" (Cotterill, 2002, p. 111) in the criminal justice system where the whole process begins—it is equally crucial and perhaps even more crucial to have access to an independent professional interpreting service. The features of police discourse, challenges of the bilingual interviewing setting, and the suggested strategies to manage these factors affecting interpreting performance will be discussed in the following chapters.

Abbreviations used in the book:

ST: Source Language
TL: Target Language
PO: Police Officer
Int: Interpreter
S/W: Suspect/Witness

1

THE INTERPRETING PROFESSION

This book is intended as a resource for professional interpreters as well as members of law enforcement agencies and other professionals who may need to conduct investigative interviews in bilingual settings. In order to understand the nature of interpreting within the police and broader legal context, it is necessary to see this in relation to what the interpreting profession is, how interpreting is done, and what skills are involved. This will help interpreter users to develop an appreciation of the level of complexity interpreting entails as well as the areas to pay attention to when assessing interpreting quality.

What Is Interpreting?

Interpreting is about communicating what is said in one language into another. Gerver (1971, p. viii, as cited in Pöchhacker, 2007, p. 16) defines interpreting as "a fairly complex form of human information processing involving the reception, storage, transformation, and transmission of verbal information," which highlights its nature of performing multiple cognitive tasks, sometimes concurrently (receiving incoming messages and holding them in the short-term memory), and, at other times, sequentially (reproducing output utterances after comprehending the input ones). In the theoretical field, there is no agreement as to whether translation is an overarching term encompassing both the written (i.e., translation proper) and oral (i.e., interpreting) transfer of meaning between two languages, or whether they should be clearly delineated based on their different forms of activities. It is no wonder that we commonly hear lay people, or even credible TV news reporters, refer to interpreters as translators—most likely a misnomer—due to a lack of understanding about the difference between the two.

Interpreters Are Like …

Many analogies have been used to describe interpreters and what they do, from "*a phonograph … a transmission belt … a bilingual transmitter*" in the legal realm (Morris, 1999, p. 8), an "*electric transformer:* (Wells, 1991, p. 329), a "*conduit of communication*" (Laster, 1990, p. 18; Laster & Taylor, 1994, p. 112; Russell, 2002, p. 117), to a "*cipher*," "*medium of communication*," or a "*language machine*" (Roberts-Smith, 2009, p. 14). There are other terms, such as a "*black box*" (Westermeyer, 1990, p. 747) and a "*cultural mediator*" (Katan, 1999, p. 12; Jalbert, 1998, as cited in Leanza, 2007, p. 14). A less flattering description of court interpreters is afforded by interpreting practitioner and academic Ruth Morris (1999, p. 7) as "*a piece of gum on the bottom of a shoe—ignored for all practical purposes, but almost impossible to remove*" (italics added). Considering how interpreting unavoidably makes things twice as long, it is no wonder that "although interpreters are essential in bilingual cases, they are not particularly liked by anyone in the courtroom. They are always seen as a necessary evil that is tolerated rather than welcomed" (Hale & Gibbons, 1999, p. 207).

Role of Interpreter

The various ways mentioned above in which interpreters are described seem to differ according to the commentator's belief in the differing extent to which interpreters should be an integral part, or otherwise, of the communicative interaction. On one end of the spectrum, analogies such as "black box" or "conduit" are made where interpreters are viewed as a linguistic machine that should not intervene in the primary speakers' dialogue. At the other end of the spectrum, terms such as *cultural mediator* or *communication facilitator* are used when interpreters are expected to intervene in the communication and play an active role to help the primary speakers achieve the desired outcome, whatever it may be. On this end of the spectrum, Roberts (2002, p. 159) recommends that interpreters should "… explain cultural differences and misunderstandings and … make explicit what may be behind the responses or decisions of the person who does not speak the official language, in order to ensure that the latter receives full and equal access to public services." Note that this view is not necessarily shared by all other practitioners and scholars, including the authors of this book.

Situated somewhere in the middle of the spectrum is the less interventionist but more interactionist approach recommended by academics such as Swedish professor Cecilia Wadensjö (1998), who asserts that, in interpreter-mediated interactions, "the meaning conveyed in and by talk is partly a joint product" (p. 8) and the interpreter takes on not only the role of language translator, but also that of an active builder and processor of speech, inevitably influencing the speech itself. Sign language interpreting educator Cynthia Roy (2000) also reminds us that in an interpreted event "all parties involved are jointly responsible, to differing degrees, for its communicative success or failure" (p. 6). Note that this middle ground in the spectrum takes a sociolinguistic approach to the interpreter's role in contributing to the construction of meaning, but neither Wadensjö nor Roy advocates any agency for the interpreter to mediate cultural or power gaps between the primary speakers, a position the authors support.

The Interpreting Process

Interpreting can be conceptually simplified as a process involving two main steps: "comprehension" of meaning expressed in one language, and "expression" of the same in another. Translation theorist Eugene Nida proposed a similar sequence: "analysis" of the source language (SL), followed by "restructuring" in the target language (TL) (as cited in Munday, 2008, p. 40). The "interpretive model" (Lederer, 2003, p. 115, as cited in Munday, 2008, p. 63), on which Nida's theory is based, interposes a third step, "deverbalization," denoting the conversion of linguistic forms to nonlinguistic ideas (i.e., meanings) in our heads before the reexpression in the TL. Whether this extra stage in the middle actually occurs or not is questioned by some academics and practitioners, because it cannot be directly observed or objectively assessed.

What Is Being Transferred Across Languages?

In most definitions and descriptions of interpreting, the focus is, and rightly so, on the transfer of meaning and sense rather than word-for-word transfer. Forensic linguist John Gibbons (2007, p. 23) reminds us that "the spoken word can survive only in memory, but memory works on the basis of meaning not wording." This highlights precisely how interpreters perform their work, relying on the meaning behind the superficial construction of lexis (i.e., words) and syntax (i.e., formation of sentences).

In most settings, interpreters work with the pragmatic meaning—what parties actually mean behind the words they say. If someone produces an utterance in English that "It is raining cats and dogs," one would not normally expect the same be expressed in the TL using exactly the same words. As translation and interpreting practitioner and scholar Sergio Viaggio (2000, p. 229) says, interpreters should "first and foremost ascertain what counts as relevance (for the speaker, for the speaker's addressees and mutually)." He describes relevance as the "propositional content [i.e., real-life meaning] conveyed by the speaker's utterance(s)" in terms of the listener, noting that this relevance "can only be assessed on the basis of and in the light of the pragmatic intentions behind it" (p. 231). So, according to Viaggio (2000), "in order to understand him, and not simply what he is saying officially, you must look behind his official discourse" (p. 231). This highlights the fact that cross-lingual communication, in most cases, orients toward achieving the pragmatic aims of the interaction, rather than adhering to a literal but nonsensical approach, unless there is a good reason to do so. Exceptions to a sense-to-sense approach in interpreting may arise on limited occasions such as in cross examination at court hearings or in police interviews. Regardless of whether it makes sense or not, the court may decide it is necessary to know the exact words used by the speaker rather than the intended meaning, so it is afforded the opportunity to determine what the intended meaning is. This point will be further discussed in Chapter 4, which covers linguistic transfer issues.

An examination of how the statement: "A $50 fine will be enforced for jaywalking," as interpreted can serve as an example of the transfer of pragmatic meaning. It may be the case that in certain

TL the statement has to be expressed as "a $50 fine will be enforced for crossing the road unlawfully" or for "not obeying road crossing rules," or a similar expression. The TL rendition may not contain the word *jaywalking* literally or in the same sentence structure, e.g., using negation ("not obeying road-crossing rules") instead of the positive sentence structure of the SL. However, no one can reasonably dispute that the communicative intent of the SL is not preserved by the TL utterance.

Choosing to express the idea of "jaywalking" as "crossing the road unlawfully" or "not obeying road-crossing rules," may be regarded by some as a kind of intervention by the interpreter. However, there may be reasons to justify this decision. For one thing, the immediacy of interpreting often requires the interpreter to concentrate on the intended meaning (communicative intent), as there is little time (compared to written translation, for example) to look for the most appropriate lexical equivalent, assuming there is one. The expectation of the parties involved in a communicative event is often that when an SL segment by one party is given, it should be expressed by the interpreter into the TL, *instantly*.

For another thing, it may be that there is no lexical equivalent, even if the interpreter has time to look for one (for example, when the speed of the talk temporarily slows down, or the speaker is interrupted by something else), because this action "jaywalking" may not have been lexicalized (put into a word) in the TL at all, or it may not be an offense in some cultures, as many travelers to different corners of the world would have experienced. These expressions may need to be interpreted using alternative strategies, such as paraphrasing or explaining or even as a drawing in order to enable comprehension between the conversing parties.

Lexis Across Languages—and Beyond

The way languages and cultures lexicalize ideas, objects, and actions basically depends on need and the need can relate to a range of factors, including traditions, beliefs, life styles, history, geographical locations, food sources, business and economy, and use of technology. With the passage of time, different generations of a particular language and culture also can lexicalize things differently because some of the factors above may have changed over time and needs may have changed accordingly, which may explain some of the communication problems even in a family home using the same language.

For example in the Arabic language, there is an extensive range of terms to refer to a camel. One of the classifications is based on drinking habits and offers at least 15 ways to name a camel (Figure 1.1).

Arabic names for camel depending on water drinking habits

A camel that drinks once every two days	الغب
A camel that drinks once every 3 days	الربع
A camel that drinks once every day, specifically at midday	الظاهرة
A camel that drinks at any time	الرفه
A camel that drinks once during the day and once at night	العريجاء
A female camel that leads other camels to the watering hole to drink	السلوف
A female camel in the middle of a herd of camels	الدفون
A female camel that gets thirsty quickly	الهافة or الملواح
A female camel that smells the water but often doesn't drink it	عيوف
A female camel that doesn't drink to heal her affliction	مقلح
A camel that returns to the watering hole to drink once more	التندية
A female camel that doesn't drink from the watering hole when it's busy, but waits and observes	رقوب
A female camel that doesn't often leave the watering hole	ملحاح
A female camel that rushes to get to the watering hole	ميراد
Thirsty camel	الهيام

Figure 1.1   Arabic names for camel depending on water drinking habits. (Retrieved from http://www.arabglot.com)

Except in those cultures based geographically in desert terrain and using camels as an integral part of the functioning of that society, no language would be expected to have lexical equivalents for all of these types of camels. As American linguist Edward Sapir (1956) observes:

> No two languages are ever sufficiently similar to be considered as representing the same social reality. The worlds in which different societies live are distinct worlds, not merely the same world with different labels attached (p. 69).

The English language is estimated to have 500,000+ words. The Turkish monolingual dictionary is said to contain approximately 100,000 words, whereas Dutch has roughly 250,000 words, just about half the number of English words. Of the Australian indigenous languages currently in use, each is said to have approximately 10,000 words (Blake, 1981). These figures may vary depending on the source and which word forms are included in the word count, but what is certain is that different languages have substantially different numbers of words. Even the same language may have varying numbers of words in its vocabulary and different ways of referring to things depending on where it is spoken geographically, as is often the case with Arabic, Mandarin Chinese, and Spanish. Even if a word exists in a number of varieties of the same language, it may be that it is used to refer to different ideas, objects, or actions, or the same object may have different words assigned to it, depending on where it is uttered geographically. A car's boot in Australian English is a car's trunk in American English, while a bonnet is a hood in American English.

This further explains, as many professional interpreters often find themselves having to explain, that a transfer of meaning cannot be achieved simply by replacing SL words with TL words. It is not a glossary matching exercise that can be automated, regardless of the attempts and efforts by ambitious corporations around the world to invent a machine or software that could make interpreters/translators redundant. A simple test by running "caught between a rock and a hard place" in Google Translate will demonstrate this point in no uncertain terms. Each word or phrase requires the interpreter to undergo a process of analyzing its communicative intent in the particular context it is used, and to weigh options available in the TL about both the intended meaning and the lexical equivalent, before the interpreter can finally settle on the best option—and this whole process takes place instantly and in the presence of the other parties involved staring at the interpreter.

Additionally, the decision-making process on the interpreter's part extends to analyzing syntactical structure (formation of sentences), which may be totally different in the TL, or even if it is similar, it may not be used as commonly or in the same context. Copying the SL syntactical structure literally, even if the lexical equivalents (words) are accurate, may lead to distortion of meaning or difficulty in comprehension. For example, in English when we refer to an address, we start from the street number, the street name, followed by the suburb and the city; and in British and Australian English, we refer to a date by starting from the date of the month, followed by the month and the year. Replicating the same order in Chinese in both cases will sound totally absurd as you need to reverse the order in the address to start from the city, then the suburb, followed by the street name and lastly the street number. The same applies to the date where the year should go first before the month and the day of the month.

One further complicating aspect of all this is that meaning does not always stay in one constant form. Different meanings may arise as a result of different factors, such as who the speakers are, the setting in which an utterance is made, and the time of the utterance. Tourism Australia's $180 million advertising campaign in 2006 using the tagline "Where the bloody hell are you?" sparked controversy in the United Kingdom—Australia's no. 1 source of inbound tourists at the time. To Tourism Australia, the slogan simply used an Australian colloquialism, whereas the U.K. Broadcasting Advertising Clearance Centre considered it offensive, citing a U.K. research study that stated 70% of respondents thought "bloody" was either mildly, fairly, or severely offensive (Gibson, 2006). Perhaps in Australia, and particularly for the younger generation, this term is no longer vulgar. However, it is a totally different story when it is used in a different place on a different population, even when that population speaks English.

Classification of Meaning

One useful classification of meaning was proposed by Mona Baker (1992). She identifies four levels of meaning:

1. Propositional meaning (real-life meaning) hit, cut, eat, walk, complain, etc. (where most obvious and serious interpreting errors occur)
2. Expressive meaning (propositional meaning plus speaker's feelings), e.g., bash, gobble, jog, dob in, chop
3. Presupposed meaning (words or expressions occurring together—collocations), e.g., take for granted, looking up a word, brush teeth, breach a code of ethics, etc.
4. Evoked meaning (dialect and register): geographic, temporal, social, e.g., teeth pop out/erupt/come through (for children)

It is unlikely that each of these levels would have exact counterparts in other languages, even in languages with similar cultural backgrounds. Again, this demonstrates the complexity of interpreting between two languages and cultures and the unrealistic nature of a typical request often heard from monolingual speaker: "Just tell me what he/she says."

How much is enough or adequate in cross-lingual communication depends on the context and the purpose at hand. For example, the sentence: "the man was pacing up and down the corridor" can be interpreted as "the man was walking up and down the corridor" and this will be sufficient in most contexts where the question was an enquiry about what physical activity the man was doing. However, the expressive meaning in "pacing up and down," which is "walking in an anxious or impatient state," according to Collins Cobuild English Language Dictionary, may be very important to capture in, say, a mental health context where "pacing up and down" may reveal the mental state of the patient. It is critical that this is conveyed by the interpreter in the TL. Leaving the expressive meaning out in this case would be an "unjustified intervention" by the interpreter in a mental health setting.

Does all this complexity mean that interpreting between two languages is impossible? Given the fact that it has been practiced for centuries throughout the world, it is no doubt possible, generally speaking, to transfer meaning using a variety of strategies and all available linguistic and cultural resources to achieve the best possible communication outcomes. There, however, may be some inevitable loss of meaning when conveying culture-specific or domain-specific terms and expressions, hence, the inevitable "lost in translation" effect—to varying degrees.

Core Competence of an Interpreter

This then brings us to what professional interpreters actually do or should be doing. Simply put, the core competence of an interpreter is *instant* comprehension and expression of *contextualized* meaning from one spoken language into another. Unlike translation (written transfer of meaning) where one does not work under the same time constraints and would have a chance to analyze, select, and review alternatives available, the emphasis here is on the immediacy of the interpreting act and the dependency of the meaning on the context, which requires that a split-second decision be made by the interpreter among a possible range of meanings that an utterance has. For example, the statement: "The reception was poor" can be a number of things: phone reception, formal welcoming, or even a wedding or engagement celebration.

All people who need professional interpreting services from time to time to go about their daily lives (e.g., seeing a doctor at the hospital) or carry out their work (e.g., taking a statement from a witness) are perfectly entitled to expect the best possible means of communicating with someone who does not speak their language, regardless of the topic area, as if the two parties spoke the same language. It is, accordingly, only natural that all parties communicating via an interpreter assume that what the interpreter said is what the other party had just before expressed. The interpreter, therefore, is expected to interpret everything that is said by the parties as accurately and as completely as possible, because both parties will be acting or making decisions on the assumption that what they heard was the utterances of the other party, not of the interpreter. It is in no small part the interpreter's responsibility to be clear about this expectation and avoid any undue distortions, omissions, or additions, or engage in any other activity that may interfere with the relationship between the two conversing parties. The authors are firmly of the view that such awareness and the conduct guided by such awareness are crucial quality indicators for professional interpreting. This will be discussed in further detail in Chapter 3.

Skills Required for Interpreting

Now that we have defined the core competency for professional interpreters, we move on to the skills required to develop such competency.

A review of the literature shows that different theorists suggest different prerequisite skills for interpreters. Interpreting practitioner and theorist Daniel Gile (1995) regards language skills, cultural expression abilities, translation skills, and memory skills as the main factors that affect the performance of interpreters. Others focus on interpersonal and intercultural skills (Frishberg, 1990; Cai & Fang, 2003). In relation to legal interpreting, an interpreter's intelligence level, language abilities, depth of legal knowledge, adaptability, and mental qualities, such as memory, judgment, concentration of attention, and dispersing ability, also are considered relevant (Kahane, 2000; Cai & Fang, 2003).

In summarizing the skills proposed by various scholars as essential for interpreters, the authors would classify them under the following headings:

- Bilingualism
- Biculturalism
- Transfer skills

Bilingualism: Language Competence

Bilingualism, for the purposes of interpreting, is the ability to converse fluently in two languages with respect to the grammar, syntax, idiomatic usage, registers, and proficiency in some or all dialects of both languages. It means having an excellent understanding of both languages and the ability to use them appropriately in a full range of contexts.

People who are bilingual, in general, tend to use their language skills one language at a time and mostly in the same context. For example, they may use their English language skills at work or at school, but, at home when speaking to their parents or undertaking cultural ceremonies, they may mostly use their other language. This means that, although they are bilingual, their skills in each language may develop differently in different contexts. A bilingual person who is familiar with legal, engineering, medical, or banking terms in English due to their work may not be as fluent in the same fields in their other language simply because they have no need to converse in the other language in such fields. In contrast, a professional interpreter working in various contexts on a daily basis must be equally fluent in both languages, covering all public service domains including the contextual areas of education, law, healthcare, and social welfare.

There is a great deal of debate among interpreting theorists as to the relationship between individual bilingualism and professional interpreting skills. In other words, to what extent does bilingualism predispose an individual to interpreting competency? Academic Mike Dillinger (1994) is critical of those who believe that interpreting requires a different set of competencies that are separate and distinct from those achieved by bilinguals:

> In most studies, it is assumed and/or asserted (without evidence) that the skills of interpreters are not characteristic of bilinguals in general, and, hence, that the models developed of skilled interpreting do not apply to novice interpreters. On this view, then, there are important, but still unidentified, differences in the ways that novice and experienced interpreters perform the task. An important implication of this view is that experience and training are of great importance because they lead to qualitative differences in how the task is carried out (p. 155).

We do not intend to overstate the unique capabilities required of professional interpreters when performing their work, as opposed to the skills possessed by bilingual nonprofessionals who might have linguistic and communicative skills. However, in the remainder of the chapter, we seek to identify what "additional" skills professional interpreters may need when working in a police and legal environment, and we highlight how these skills are unique even in the wider interpreting sphere.

Biculturalism: Cultural/Contextual Knowledge

Culture and language are interwoven. Any discussion of either one will inevitably involve the other. Therefore, an interpreter has to be not only fluent in the languages in which he/she interprets, but also familiar with the underlying cultural issues that determine meaning in particular contexts. Knowledge of culture for interpreting purposes includes not just customs and traditions, but also the governmental, administrative, legal, economic, social, and educational systems of both cultures involved in the interpreting situation.

We can narrow essential bicultural knowledge further in the case of police/legal interpreting to the following:

- A sound knowledge of the legal and criminal justice systems and processes.
- A sound knowledge of legal discourse including register, collocations, and jargon
- An understanding of the expectations, work practices and methods, and role boundaries of the legal professionals and institutions, and how to work professionally with them

It may be possible to reach a level of language competence in both languages that is sufficient to undertake professional interpreting to a minimum standard. However, it can be argued that acquiring contextual knowledge in both cultures is an ongoing process as many systems, institutions, practices, and procedures continuously undergo changes and an interpreter is expected to keep abreast of these changes.

It must be emphasized, though, that the cultural competency we discuss here is meant to assist fundamental interpreting processes of comprehension and expression, rather than providing cultural advice/consultancy, particularly in the case of interpreting, to the other professional involved in the interpreted event. In everyday practice, interpreters are faced with situations where the professional (e.g., doctor, social worker, police officer, lawyer) he/she interprets for poses questions to them, rather than to the client speaking another language, about cultural issues perceived by the professional during the interpreted event. Interpreters need to be wary of giving cultural advice unless it is required to clear a breakdown in communication. This aspect will be discussed in more detail in Chapter 3 on the professional role boundary and conduct issues of which interpreters must be aware.

Transfer Skills

Possessing the bilingual and bicultural skills described above does not automatically make one an interpreter. As already noted, a bilingual person is normally fluent in speaking one language independent of the other in a particular application (e.g., at home, for study, or for work), and vice versa. Crossing over to the other language back and forth in one communicative event on a specialized topic area may not be every bilingual person's cup of tea and may indeed be beyond that person's capabilities. This calls for a high level of verbal transfer skills, which is what defines an interpreter. Ultimately, an interpreter is someone who is able to comprehend *contextualized meaning* in the SL and express the same in the TL *instantly*, and he/she keeps going in and out of his/her pair of languages continuously within one communicative event.

Modes of Interpreting

There are two modes of interpreting from the point of view of the timing when output utterances are produced by the interpreter in relation to input messages uttered by the primary speakers who do not share the same language in one communicative event: simultaneous interpreting and consecutive interpreting (Danks, Shreve, Fountain, & McBeath, 1997; Gile, 2009). Simultaneous interpreting is often used in sign language interpreting or, for spoken language, seen at international conferences where spoken-language interpreters (normally in pairs working in the same combination of languages) interpret as the speech is delivered on the podium via audio equipment to the audience wearing earphones in order that they understand instantly the speech in their own language. Therefore, this form of interpreting also is known as conference interpreting. A variation of simultaneous interpreting is sometimes seen in settings such as in a courtroom or tribunal where no equipment is involved, but the interpreter renders the interpretation in a lowered voice to the person seated next to him/her who needs to understand what is being said at the bench or by the judge. This form of simultaneous interpreting is known as whisper interpreting, or *chuchotage* in French.

In most community-interpreting contexts, where delivering public service is the prime purpose, interpreting is normally done in a
triadic setup. This situation, from an interactional point of view, is
manifestly dialogic. The service provider speaks through an interpreter to the person, who does not speak the same language, receiving
that service. This is normally carried out in the same physical space
(e.g., in a doctor's office) or via audio-visual equipment (e.g., by telephone or video conferencing unit). Interpreting is rendered, normally
within a few seconds, when the professional or the client pauses after
uttering a few sentences. These professional–interpreter–client and
client–interpreter–professional sequences go on continuously until the
conversation between the professional and the client is completed.
At any given time, there is only one person talking, and the other
participants listening. And there is always one party that does not
understand what the others are talking about. This form of interpreting is referred to as *consecutive interpreting*. Considering the interactive
nature of community interpreting in the consecutive mode, it also is
commonly referred to as *dialogue interpreting*.

Another application of consecutive interpreting is seen in settings
such as speeches or public addresses to audiences where the speakers
go on for a few minutes, pause for the interpreter to interpret, and
then resume talking. This sequence keeps repeating until the speech
is complete.

A hybrid mode of interpreting seen in various community interpreting settings should be mentioned here as well. Interpreters may
be given a written document during the assignment and will be asked
to provide an instant oral translation of the content in the document.
Such a document might be, for example, a dietary information sheet
from the diabetes nurse, or, in legal settings, an intervention order
handed down by the magistrate, bail conditions set out by a bail justice, or a statement just typed by the interviewing police officer based
on what the witness just said. This form of mixed-mode interlingual
operation from written text to oral reexpression in another language
is referred to as *sight translation*. Professional interpreters must be able
to interpret in all modes of interpreting and be able to switch between
different modes when circumstances demand.

The Professional Role of Interpreters in Legal Settings

The role played by interpreters in legal settings, in particular in court and police interviews, is generally expected by the primary speakers to be that of a conduit or a mouthpiece. The reason for this is that interpreted questions and responses in the exchange are included in evidence as having been made by these parties, not by the interpreter. The other roles often attributed to interpreters, such as cultural mediators or facilitators (Tipton, 2010; Anderson, 1976; 2002), essentially allowing interpreters to undertake such extra tasks as giving advice or making suggestions or managing a conversation between the conversing parties, do not apply when interpreting in legal and police settings.

Interpreters are essentially bound by the legal relationship between the parties. This preexisting relationship between the parties, therefore, draws the boundaries within which an interpreter is able to move. It is essential for an interpreter to respect the preexisting relationship between the clients and not engage in any activity that may interfere with this relationship. Ways in which an interpreter can interfere with a preexisting professional–client relationship may include:

- Giving advice or information
- Explaining information
- Giving any instruction that is not part of the transfer process
- Taking control of the interview in any other way
- Providing their own opinion, or even diagnosis
- Unjustified omission or addition of information
- Distorting meaning
- Allowing personal opinion or views to affect their interpreting

Various studies have demonstrated that interpreters in formal settings do become active agents in helping the client speaking another language to construct narratives that are needed by the interviewers or they offer their advice out of their own cultural frames, rather than merely rendering SL utterances into the TL. For example, in a 2004 report examining the practice of interpreting in healthcare settings in the Australian state of Queensland, the authors cite testimony from a domestic violence refuge worker who worked with an interpreter who "told the woman's [i.e., the victim's] husband the address of the women's shelter; she thought the woman was lying and, therefore, her husband needed to know" (CHAG, p. 25). In one case, an interpreter "tried to convince the woman [i.e., her client] to reconcile with her husband," and, in other cases, interpreters "criticized women for taking legal action" (p. 747). While no single study collates evidence of the nature and extent of these kinds of unwarranted interpreter interventions in professional work in Australia or elsewhere, there is frequent reference to such problems in the secondary literature. For example, there is a reported case of a female interpreter who interrupted a therapeutic counseling session to advise the client that, according to the Koran, women must obey their husbands' sexual demands (Allimant, Martinez, & Wong, 2006, p. 160). Another case notes a male interpreter intervening in a family court proceeding to explain that, in Arab culture, it is acceptable for a man to refuse to participate in a parenting course on the basis that such courses are "for women." In this case, the interpreter's male client was objecting to a family court order (Hale, 2007, pp. 141–142). It must be highlighted that this interpreter's actions on the basis that the "culture" the interpreter refers to is a male-centered one that does not necessarily represent people of all Arab backgrounds (pp. 141–142).

It is not uncommon for parties in legal/police settings to claim that they have been disadvantaged because of a particular interpretation afforded in the police interview or at a hearing in court due to lexical choices or a particular conduct issue, such as those described above. When interpreting quality is raised as an issue by one of the parties during the legal process, the interpreter involved may be subpoenaed as a witness to appear in court so he/she can be asked to state under oath/affirmation that he/she interpreted accurately to the best of his/her skills and ability, or to give evidence about any linguistic or conduct issues raised, and he/she also can be cross examined.

A Case in Point—Katsuno et al. v. Australia (2006)   On June 17, 1992, a group of Japanese nationals were arrested at Melbourne Airport and charged with the importation of heroin for commercial purposes. They were initially interviewed by Customs officers and subsequently by the Australian Federal Police with the assistance of interpreters. On May 28, 1994, a jury at the County Court in Melbourne found them guilty of the charges and imposed custodial terms ranging from 15 to 25 years. The defendants appealed to the Court of Appeal of the Supreme Court of Victoria, but only one of them was granted a retrial, which again returned a guilty verdict. Subsequent appeals for leave to appeal to the Court of Appeal of the Supreme Court of Victoria in 1997 and the High Court of Australia in 1999 were denied. The members of the group lodged an application (CCPR/C/88/d/1154/2003) with the UN Human Rights Committee in 2002 claiming violations of their rights under Articles 2, 9, 14, and 26 of the International Covenant on Civil and Political Rights. Among other things, the members of the group alleged that several interpreting errors had led to their wrongful conviction and imprisonment. They claimed that interpreters:

1. wrongly or very inaccurately interpreted the investigator's questions/defendant's answers;
2. failed to interpret questions asked by the investigator;
3. arbitrarily asked their own questions of the defendants;
4. provided answers that the defendants simply did not give;
5. provided erroneous explanations to the investigator about the social meaning of Japanese terms;
6. provided answers in English that, in some cases, were grammatically and syntactically deficient and, in others, were simply unintelligible English utterances;
7. conducted long exchanges in Japanese with the applicants, in which the investigator did not participate, and then simply summarized, often inaccurately, what had transpired; and
8. were unable to translate key legal terms. (UN CCPR, 2006)

The above list includes examples of many of the common issues associated with poor interpreting performance in general. Items 1, 6, and 8 can be categorized as linguistic transfer issues and the rest relate to nonlinguistic transfer issues or professional conduct issues by interpreters. (Also see *Katsuno et al. v. Australia 2006* under subheading Interpreter Competency in the Introduction.)

Summary

In this chapter, we have given an introduction to what interpreting is, what skills are required for professional interpreters, and the unique role interpreters play within any given job context, therefore, guiding what their linguistic resources and ethical conduct should be. In the following chapter, we shall move on to explain more specifically what investigative interviewing in the law enforcement context is, in order to set the foundation for further discussions on professional interpreting taking place in such contexts.

2

INVESTIGATIVE INTERVIEWING

… the investigative task is the core aspect of policing today and
what emerges from that core task is the key element of the ability
to interview

G. Evans and M. Webb
(1993, p. 37)

This chapter is an introduction to Investigative Interviewing, a
growing field from the 1970s in a range of areas including psychology, insurance investigation, market research interviews,
workplace investigations, and police investigative interviews with
victims, witnesses, and suspects. Three areas of particular interest
have been the significance of rapport building, verbal and nonverbal communication techniques for successful interviews, and
strategies available to interviewers.

Introduction

The basic premise of investigative interviewing is to elicit as much
information as possible from an interviewee without resorting to coercion or deception. Because this book is about interpreter-mediated
investigative interviews in police and other law enforcement settings
(e.g., customs and border security), this chapter will introduce readers
to major investigative interviewing models and the relevant concepts,
strategies, and applications.

The Significance of Investigative Interviews

There are various occasions when police officers need to speak to people in the community to obtain information that cannot be obtained from other sources. These include talking to victims or witnesses of crimes, persons of interest in an investigation, or at information sessions for community members. A survey conducted by police researchers McGurk, Carr, and McGurk (1993) found firstly that interviewing of witnesses and suspects is in the top four of the most frequently conducted tasks in day-to-day policing, and, secondly, from the point of view of police officers, their three most important investigative duties are taking statements, interviewing witnesses, and interviewing suspects.

Police interviews, therefore, are regarded as "goal-focused events, the primary aim of which is the collection and synthesis of evidence into a written statement for use in any subsequent court hearing" (Coulthard & Johnson, 2007, p. 80). James Stewart, director of the U.S. National Institute of Justice, highlights the significance of police interviews in the elicitation of crucial information:

> Information is the lifeblood of criminal investigation and it is the ability of investigators to obtain useful and accurate information from witnesses and victims of crime that is crucial to effective law enforcement (cited in Geiselman & Fisher, 1985, p. 1)

Interviews may be recorded in a police statement, containing a narrative written up by the interviewing officers from the answers to the questions posed to the interviewees. The matters under investigation may range from relatively minor offenses, such as driving infringements, all the way up to serious crimes, such as murder. In Australia, police interviews concerning indictable offenses must be recorded using an audio or video recording device, the procedure of which must follow strict guidelines regulating police conduct and the discourse of the interview.

How victims and suspects are questioned has an impact on the outcome of the interview and the investigation. Two main models of investigative interviewing and the relevant techniques will be discussed in further detail below in the section Lexical Choice. Suffice it to say that inappropriate interviewing tactics, among other things, have contributed to false confessions, leading to wrongful convictions, and, thus, to miscarriages of justice (Gudjonsson, 2003, pp. 445–457; Carrabine, Cox, Lee, Plummer, & South, 2013, p. 260). The dire consequences of poor interviewing should be avoided at all costs, as is aptly put by British police researchers Milne and Bull (1999):

> Society cannot afford investigative interviewing to be poor. This affects people's perceptions of the criminal justice system. The guilty get away, the innocent convicted, justice for children and vulnerable adults is inadequate. Poor interviewing is of no value to anyone; it is a waste of time, resources, and money. No one wins. People will not come forward if they have no confidence in the quality of investigators' interviewing techniques (p. 191).

Interviewing Skills of Police Officers

Police officers must possess interview skills in order to conduct effective interviews. An interviewer should be formally trained so that he/she is "easy to talk to through the appropriate use of vocal inflection, modulation, and emphasis; is able to convey appropriate emotional responses at various times as needed (e.g., sympathy, anger, fear, and joy); is impartial, flexible and open minded; and knows how to use psychology, salesmanship, and dramatics" (Swanson, Chamelin, & Territo, 2002, as cited in Schollum, 2005, p. 16).

The England and Wales Central Police Training and Development Authority's Centrex training material (National Crimes and Operations Faculty, 2003) identifies four core skills a police officer ideally should develop:

1. The ability to plan and prepare for interviews
2. The ability to establish rapport
3. Effective listening
4. Effective questioning

When Interpreters Are Needed

In multilingual societies, the questioning strategies and techniques employed by the interviewing police officer have to be "routed" through an interpreter in cases where the parties speak different languages. Trained police interviewers use particular types of wording and questions in order to elicit uncontaminated information from the interviewee. Their lexical choices are by no means accidental and, therefore, must be maintained in their entirety as much as possible in the Target Language (TL) by the interpreter.

Of the four core skills in the Centrex training manual mentioned above, the second (establishing rapport) and fourth (developing effective questioning) skills often have to be applied through the use of language. As a result, where an interpreting service is called for, the application of these two skills may be open to intervention, justified or unjustified, by the interpreter. This is where the authors advocate the training in police interviewing and police interpreting should intersect. However, a search of the Internet shows that in countries, such as Australia, Canada, the United Kingdom, and the United States, no training programs or professional development activities for interpreters can be found that cover the introduction of professional interpreters to police interviewing models or their relevant questioning techniques. On the other hand, issues about working with people who have language barriers or different cultural backgrounds are increasingly recognized by law enforcement agencies in mainly multilingual countries in the West. Police training courses in these countries increasingly include content on cultural and linguistic awareness.* However, they appear to cover broader cross-cultural communication issues or protocols on working with interpreters. There appears to be a lack of specialized training that better equips police in conducting major investigative interviews through interpreters.

---

* Good practice, as carried out by the Police Academy of the Netherlands, offers detectives the training for professional investigative interviewing. Within this training, 36 hours are dedicated to the subject of relevant third parties being present during the (preparation of) the interview (e.g., lawyer, specific expert, or interpreter). Separately, 8 hours are dedicated to interpreter-related topics with an aim to gain knowledge about legal prescriptions and different modes of interpreting; to become aware of the interpreter's job, the possible effects of an interpreter being present, and to be able to handle those effects; and the importance of briefing the interpreter (personal communication with reviewer of this book, 2014).

Impact of Interpreting on Questioning Strategies Used By Police

When police interview children as witnesses or victims in the state of Victoria, Australia, they must comply with the video or audio taping of evidence (VATE) legislation. Forensic linguist Georgina Heydon (2005, p. 162) reports that questions worded using:

"Can you describe to/for me ...?"

elicit substantial responses, whereas:

"Do you know ...?"

or

"Can you remember ... ?"

kinds of questions are less likely to achieve the same. Similarly, the 2004 New Zealand Police guidelines recommend the use of TED questions as follows when interviewing children and vulnerable witnesses.

Tell me ...
Can you explain to me ...
Can you describe to me ...

The same guidelines also recommend the use of *"How come ..."* questions instead of *"Why ..."* questions when dealing with children and vulnerable witnesses, as this phrase is regarded as less accusatory and exerts a different impact on witnesses.

These recommendations were the subject of a study conducted by two authors of this book (Lai & Mulayim, 2013) in bilingual settings of 11 commonly used community languages in Melbourne, Australia. The study used two mock police interview scripts as research tools, incorporating the TED and "how come" questions; 11 experienced practicing professional interpreters were recruited and asked to interpret the mock interviews in laboratory settings. The study results show that expressions using the TED questions were all conveyed accurately by all the interpreters in the intended meaning using the same wording in their respective TL. However, expressions using the "how come" questions were interpreted using the equivalent form in the TLs on only 45% of the occasions. All 11 languages in the study, through unstructured interviews after the experiment, are able to produce a linguistic equivalent, or a similar one, to express the less accusatory "how come" questions (as opposed to "why" questions, e.g., *How come* you took the item without paying for it?" versus "*Why* did you take the item without paying for it?"). As the study shows, it is more likely (55%) than not that the deliberate choice of wording ("how come" rather than "why") is interfered with by unknowing interpreters who achieved meaning transfer, but changed the style of wording to a more accusatory one. The authors wish to point out, though, that in languages other than the 11 tested in the study, there will likely be ones that lack linguistic equivalents to reproduce the same distinction in formality, i.e., a more and a less accusatory form of questioning. This no doubt complicates the issue and only through further collaborative research and mutual understanding of the police and interpreting professions can better insights be gained as to what can and cannot be achieved in bilingual police interviewing.

When conducting interpreting across languages, or "interlingual" interpreting (Jakobson, 1959), interpreters must attend to the meaning (i.e., what is said) as well as the form and style (i.e., how things are said). Significant linguistic features other than meaning, for example, the choice of words (although the meaning might be the same), the order of ideas (although the ideas might be the same), and altered sentence structure (creating marked expression although the words might be the same as the unmarked expression) are all integral parts of language communication. When analyzing interlingual interpreting, as is the case in written translation, a literal approach, based on the form of the source language (SL) (or sometimes referred to as word-for-word) and a free approach, based on the meaning of the SL (or sometimes referred to as sense-for-sense), often represent the two extremes of the spectrum. In the area of legal and police interpreting, due to the rules of evidence and legal implications, legal professionals have made clear their preference for receiving literal interpretation, leaving themselves to do what they do best—"interpreting" the law. Note that the interpreting here carried out by legal professionals, as opposed to that carried out by language interpreters, is to apply and explain the law using the same language. It is, therefore, a kind of "intralingual" interpreting (Jakobson, 1959).

Main Features of Police Discourse

Often the language used in the police interviewing process, in particular, the beginning and ending of an interview, including lexical items and grammatical structures, are dictated by legislation and police regulations (Heydon, 2005). For example, the police caution administered in Australia (similar to the Miranda rights in the United States) preceding an official interview with a suspect in a criminal matter can go as follows:

PO (police officer): Before I do this I **must** inform you that you are **not obliged** to say or do anything, but anything you say or do **may be given** in evidence. Do you understand that? (Italics added) (Heydon, 2005, p. 5)

These utterances not only sound formulaic (in order to satisfy the regulations), but also exert institutional power with the use of the words in italics. Forensic linguist John Gibbons (1990, pp. 234–235) analyzes a corpus of second language speakers in police interviews and provides the following summary to highlight the issues caused by the complex language used by police interviewers:

(1.) The accumulation of phrase and constituents: the length, e.g., PO: As I have already explained to you/I am making enquiries in relation to the death of R. Z./in the early hours/of the morning/of the fourth of February, 1985,/in the vicinity/of the Mob of Cows Hotel,/Pyrmont Bridge Road,/Glebe Point Park.

There are as many as nine constituents in this sentence (separated by the forward slashes), and six prepositional phrases (underlined). On top of that, the use of police jargon, such as "in relation to" (instead of simply "about") and "in the vicinity of" (instead of "near") added to the complexity. Utterances this long and complicated make it difficult to understand, even for a native speaker.

(2.) The intricacy of grammatical relations between clauses, e.g., PO: "I want you to understand that you are not obliged to say anything unless you wish, but whatever you say will be recorded … and may be used in evidence."

Dissecting this sentence, we will find that it contains two indirect speech forms (i.e., "I want you to understand that you ..., but whatever you ... .").

(3.) Grammatical metaphor and abstract language, e.g., PO: "... prior to the **commencement** of this interview ..."; and PO: "Do you agree that I also told you at the **conclusion** of the interview you would be **given the opportunity** of reading through the interview..."?

"Commencement" in the first example and "conclusion" in the second example are noun constructions used to replace simple verbs, such as "begin" and "finish," and the passive voice in the second example, "given the opportunity" permits omission of the agent "I" (will give you the opportunity to ...), making the sentences sound more complex than necessary, particularly to a second language speaker.

(4.) Low frequency words, expressions, and grammatical structures: No examples are provided in Gibbons' (1990) paper. However, this category can easily be found in the "copspeak" in TV cop shows, where the simple words *men/women* are turned into *male persons/female persons*; a suspect is *conveyed,* instead of *taken,* to the police station for questioning; and instead of asking a person why he "took" the items from the shop without paying, the person has "removed" the items from the shop. Worse still, a simple construction of "the guy got shot and he was dead" can become "he was hit by a projectile from a high-powered weapon, numerous times until his bodily functions ceased" (Gibbons, 2007, p. 86).

1. Semantically difficult grammatical relations such as those in the passive voice and expressions such as "unless," e.g.,

PO: Do you agree that I also told you at the **conclusion** of the interview you would **be given the opportunity** of reading through the interview ... (same example from under item 3); and
PO: I want you to understand that you are not obliged to say anything **unless** you wish ... (bold type added; same example from under item 2).

All of these features of police talk may be foreign to most members of the public at the best of times. It understandably presents substantial challenges for community members who do not speak the mainstream language, or are not native speakers of it. This, in turn, gives rise to challenges to interpreters when their service is called for and they are faced with such police discourse. Interpreters must have an understanding of these features of "copspeak" in order to perform competently in the police interviewing setting.

Power Asymmetry

Police are the principal agents of social control and police power is regarded as "a mechanism for the distribution of situationally justified force by society" (Bittner, 1970, p. 39). This form of institutionally defined social control gives rise to power asymmetry in investigative interviews conducted by police, manifesting explicitly in the "forms of turn taking" and "topic management" (Heydon, 2005). The power imbalance inherent in police interviews as a type of institutional discourse is summed up well in the following:

> In police interviews with suspects, the role of each participant is clearly defined and restrained. Yet these roles are very unequal, especially in terms of the distribution of power and control. In addition to the asymmetric dynamic created by the ascribed roles of questioner and responder, the police have a considerable degree of direct power over the interviewee, controlling the setting in which the interview takes place and having the capability to make vital decisions about the interviewee's liberty and future based on the outcome ... (Haworth, 2006, p. 740).

The imbalance of power manifests itself not only in police authority over managing the whole interview process, but also in the language used. Given that language is often used as a tool to exert authority in all kinds of power relationships, it is natural for us to question what happens in "unequal encounters where the nonpowerful people have cultural and linguistic backgrounds different from those of the powerful people" (Fairclough, 1989, p. 47). On this subject, Australian legal practitioner and academic Kathy Laster (1990) offers the following observation:

> ... the linguistic tricks employed by police in an interview are probably not dissimilar from those employed in courtroom cross-examination.

But because police interviews are conducted in private, there is no "umpire" to ensure that the questioner remains within accepted procedural parameters, and there is the implicit and sometimes explicit possibility of coercion of various sorts to enlist the cooperation of the non-English speaker (p. 25).

One might argue that in countries like Australia, Britain, and many other western countries, police procedures mandate the offer of contacting a lawyer before the interview starts. Although no statistics are available on the take-up rates of such an offer, anecdotal evidence and the authors' experience suggest that more likely than not, suspects with a language barrier do not take up the offer either because they are unaware of the implications of having or not having a legal representative present during the interview in terms of safeguarding their legal rights, or they simply worry that they are unable to afford one. Not understanding what is said or being unable to express oneself fully inevitably results in a power asymmetry. In this situation, an independent and publicly funded professional interpreter often becomes the only "lifeline" for a suspect or witness who has a language barrier to comprehend the high-stakes event unfolding in front of him/her.

Interpreters, therefore, should be acutely aware of the important role they play in the police interview setting, where their act serves to bring the power dynamics to a level where an interviewee who has a language barrier is at no more of a disadvantage than a native speaker in such a setting. This can only be done when an interviewee can understand everything that is said and expresses precisely what he/she intends to say with the help of the interpreter.

Primary versus Secondary Reality

As in the courtroom setting, the process of police investigation and questioning has two layers of reality (Gibbons, 2007, pp. 78–79): the primary reality, relating to the physical environment and context, and the secondary reality, relating to the matter under investigation. Interpreters must be aware of the intertwining realities the speakers in the interpreted event are referring to, and interpret them accurately. Consider the following conversation at a police station between a police officer and a shopkeeper who has come to report a robbery that has just happened at his shop:

PO: I hope you are feeling better now. After all, it is pretty frightening to be in the situation, particularly when the guy had a gun. *(primary reality in police station)* Now, I would like you to think back from when the robber entered the shop and yelled at you. What can you tell me about what happened? *(secondary reality framing to prompt the eyewitness for information)*

S/W (suspect/witness): Well, it was about 11 o'clock and I was about to shut the shop. This guy came in the store and walked around the aisles for a few rounds. I thought he was trying to find something. So, I yelled at him, "do you need help?" *(secondary reality recounting the robbery).*

PO: How far away was he from where you stood? *(secondary reality framing for further information)*

S/W: (looks around) Not sure. About from here to where that window is. *(secondary reality using physical environment from primary reality)**

The following schema demonstrates the alternating realities of a police interview starting from the preamble and formal police caution, moving on to the actual interviewing stage, and ending with the closing statement (Gibbons, 2007, p. 142):

Primary reality framing
(Place) (Date) Time of interview
Persons present
Interviewee's Name (Address) (Date of Birth)
Police Caution
Right to silence
Recording
(Interpreter present if needed)
Secondary reality
Orientation
Subject of interview
(Date and time of incident)
Questioning

---

* This example is adopted from Gibbons (2007, p. 152).

Question–answer
(Introduction of evidence from Secondary Reality)
(Invitation to give further evidence)
Primary reality framing
Recording issues
Cautions
Uncoerced interview
(Invitation to sign)
(Further actions)
Closure (Time)

Interpreters must be clear in their minds about two things here. Firstly, they must know and understand the sequence of this formal interview process. Secondly, they must understand the questioning process, which moves backward and forward between the primary and secondary realities, in order to be able to understand what the questions and framings are alluding to. This understanding will be particularly helpful in constructing the TL expressions using the right tense and/or time references.

Lexical Choice

Police discourse is regarded as a "legal subgenre" (Coulthard & Johnson, 2007, p. 40) and may at times be challenging to lay native speakers. It is without doubt even more difficult for nonnative speakers who come from different cultural and linguistic backgrounds. On the lexical level, words are chosen carefully as part of the questioning strategy used by the police, and, later, if contested in court, by the legal counsels on both sides.

Danet (1980) talks about the construction of alternative versions of the same reality through different word choices, which is often played out in a court of law by opposing parties in an adversarial legal system. To illustrate this point, she gave the example of a high profile U.S. abortion case, in which an unborn child was referred to as a fetus by the defendant, whereas the prosecution used terms such as "loved one," "baby boy," "the deceased." and "victim." Interpreters must always be alert to the vocabulary their clients choose to use and relay the different negative–neutral–positive connotation the lexical item intends to evoke. How would terms, such as terrorist–guerilla–freedom fighter (Gibbons, 2007, p. 118) be translated into other languages considering these can be terms used to describe the same person, but from different viewpoints? Or, as discussed in Chapter 1, in the section Lexis Across Languages—and Beyond, how would we express in English the types of camel according to their drinking patterns? Interpreters must always reflect on and understand the different realities and nuances in the different cultures and linguistic systems they have to deal with in order to be able to make the appropriate choices in interlingual transfer.

It also is important to note that the transfer of one single word from one language into another can sometimes tip the balance of a legal case, and even destroy it. In October 2011, the New South Wales (Australia) District Court had to abort a people-smuggling jury trial because the interpreter was alleged to have interpreted "did you *stop* anyone moving" as "did you *push* anyone" (Jacobsen, 2011); and in April 2012, a judge in a London crown court had to order a retrial, costing the taxpayer £25,000, because it was discovered that the Romanian defendant giving evidence said the claimant had "beaten them," but the interpreter said they were "bitten" (BBC *News*, 2012). In the latter case, it was confirmed that the interpreter made the mistake but kept quiet about it, whereas it is unknown what really happened in the process of interpreting in the former case. As we know how costly it is to abort a trial and to run a retrial, the best policy for an interpreter, when realizing he/she has made a mistake, is to raise it immediately in order for parties involved to work out the impact and take mitigating or correcting measures at the earliest possible time. This is not only significant in a trial situation, but also in police interviewing and, indeed, any setting.

Produced for a Third Party

A significant aspect of police interviews, and arguably the most distinguishing aspect of the police interpreting setting as opposed to other common settings, such as interpreting in a conference or medical consultation, is that the talk is knowingly produced for a third party, or, as termed by Cotterill (2002, p. 124), for "a future audience," i.e., one of a range of members of the judicial system, just as news interviews are produced for an audience (Heritage, 1985; Greatbatch 1988, as cited in Heydon, 2005, p. 39). The third party, e.g., magistrates, judges, juries, prosecutors, barristers, will critically analyze (often with a magnifying glass), review, and interpret (intralingually) what is said, meant, and intended by the parties, and identify probable different (intralingual) interpretations of utterances. Whereas in other common settings in which interpreters work, such as health, education, business, or conference, the interactions between the parties involved are not produced for or subject to the scrutiny of a future third party.

From a sociolinguistics point of view, one of the typical constructions of a normal conversation between two people is that one person produces the first round object—the question—followed by the other person's second round object—the answer. Additionally, a third round object is often produced by the first person (asking the question) to indicate news receipts (e.g., "oh"), to add newsmarks (e.g., "did she?"), or to give assessments (e.g., "good") (Heritage, 1985, p. 98). In a police questioning sequence in an ideal setting, the interviewing police officer normally produces first round objects, followed by the interviewee's second round objects. As is the case with TV interviews, police interviewers do not customarily produce third round objects as occurs in other dialogues, such as daily conversation. The use of third round objects is considered to demonstrate the questioning officer's identification of his/her role (in the conversation) with the "news recipient" (in this case, relevant members of the judicial system), which is regarded as not appropriate and used sparingly unless they intend to achieve something else, e.g., establishing rapport with the interviewee. In general, the police interviewer attempts to maintain a neutral role alignment by avoiding responses that constitute positive or negative assessments of the news received from the interviewee (Greatbatch, 1988; Heritage, 1985; Atkinson, 1992).

Turn-Taking

The police interview shares with other institutional interviews a basic turn-taking system consisting of sequences of questions and answers (Greatbatch, 1988; Heritage, 1985; Levinson, 1992; Peräkylä & Silverman,

1991) as well as a turn pre-allocation system whereby questions are allocated to interviewers and responses to interviewees (Peräkylä & Silverman 1991; Frankel 1990).

In a conversation between two or more parties, a "turn" refers to the time when a participant in the talk is speaking and the content of it. A turn can range from one sound (e.g., *A-ha*) or one word (e.g., *Sure*) to a sentence, many sentences, a paragraph, or beyond until the next participant gets to talk. The social organization of turn-taking in naturally occurring conversations is observed by sociologists Harvey Sacks, Emanuel A. Schegloff, and Gail Jefferson (1974, pp. 700–701) and they assert, among other things, that:

- turn order is not fixed, but varies;
- turn size is not fixed, but varies;
- length of conversation is not specified in advance;
- relative distribution of turns is not specified in advance; and
- turn-allocation techniques are obviously used. A current speaker may select a next speaker (as when he addresses a question to another party), or parties may self-select in starting to talk.

From the forensic linguistics point of view, "conversations" in police interview settings, for example, manifest completely different organizational norms to the above, as is observed by Coulthard and Johnson (2007, p. 32) in that such things as "order and distribution of turns and the degree" are different. For "conversations" in other contexts, e.g., between couples, friends, or work colleagues, there tends to be equal distribution of turns in the question and answer sequences per participant, although the proportion of talk time occupied by the participants is different, depending on who intends to achieve what within the conversation. However, in police interviews, where there is power asymmetry between the interviewing officer and the person being interviewed (see Power Asymmetry), questions are invariably asked by the interviewing officer and the interviewee is expected to provide answers to those questions. The interviewee can, notwithstanding, ask questions. However, they would most likely be confined to clarifying questions put to them in the first place. Whether these questions are answered or ignored would depend on the interviewing officer's judgment of their relevance to the interview. After the opening formalities (i.e., recording preamble and police caution) are completed, the interviewing officer moves on to the information collecting stage with the aim of eliciting as much information as possible in relation to the investigation at hand. This is normally achieved by posing a series of open-ended questions, and the interviewee is encouraged to provide as detailed an answer as possible. The turn-taking features of this part of the interview are manifestly different from the ones for normal social conversations proposed by Sack, Schegloff, and Jefferson (1974) listed above. The differences can be contrasted as follows:

- Turn order is relatively fixed, with questions often allocated to the interviewing officer and answers often to the interviewee.
- Turn size is relatively fixed, with shorter turns for the interviewing officer and longer turns for the interviewees.
- Length of conversation, although not specified in advance, is predominantly determined by the interviewing officer as to when it can be terminated or when a follow-up interview is to be scheduled.
- Relative distribution of turns is specified by default of the setting.
- Turn-allocation techniques are not used by all participants in the interview, in the sense that, if the current speaker is the interviewing officer, he/she does have full access to selecting the next speaker. However, the interviewee has limited access to self-select in starting to talk.

It must be pointed out, though, that the above features of police interviews are by no means absolute. Rather, these represent more of an ideal of what police interviewers aim to achieve in their investigative interviews, and any deviation from these patterns may induce police officers to attempt to fix them and steer the dynamics back to the preferred turn-taking procedures.

Having an understanding of these turn-taking features helps the interpreter to appreciate the interviewing dynamics and better anticipate the turn lengths of each speaker, which helps their decision to initiate interruptions in order to render the interpretation of the utterances. In the case of the police interviewer, it is more likely than not that the turn lengths will be shorter and vice versa for the interviewee. Therefore, the interpreter will anticipate interrupting perhaps more times when interpreting the interviewee's utterances, keeping in mind that the interviewee should not be interrupted more often than is absolutely necessary.

Highly Prescriptive Opening and Closing

The opening and closing segments of the police interview are used to inform suspects of their rights and obligations so that all the institutional requirements are met. To comply with the highly prescriptive opening and closing formalities is extremely important on the police interviewer's part and on the interpreter's part in the case of bilingual interviews. If these parts of the interview are not done properly, it will weaken the legitimacy of the interview as evidence in court (Heydon, 2005).

It is worthwhile for interpreters to understand the conversational "role" (Goffman, 1981) of the police interviewer when making the formal opening and ending statements in an investigative interview is different from the role he/she takes during the actual interview. Using Canadian sociolinguist Erving Goffman's participation framework, we can see that these opening and ending statements are not written or constructed by the individual officers. Instead, the police interviewers utter the statements on behalf of the police institution, which bears the *authorship* and takes responsibility for the consequences (*principalship*) of these utterances. Therefore, we can compare the police officer to a sounding box for the institution he/she works for, and the only conversational role he/she takes up in the beginning and ending parts of an interview is, in Goffman's term, that of an *animator* (Heydon, 2005). The interpreter's appreciation of the role the interviewing officer has in the beginning and ending statements of an interview will help them look beyond the unusual wording and make sure their rendering of the statement is complete and accurate so they do not cause the interview to be inadmissible as evidence should the case proceed further in the criminal justice system.

Two Major Police Interview Models

In the field of investigative interviewing, there are two main interviewing models in the world: the PEACE model and the Reid technique. The PEACE model was developed by the U.K. Home Office in the 1990s and has since been used by the police forces in England

and Wales, adopted by other countries in Europe, and incorporated in training manuals to various degrees in some Australian states and in New Zealand. This model satisfies courts in countries, such as Australia and the United Kingdom where evidence obtained by oppressive police practice is not admissible. In contrast, the earliest origin of the Reid Technique can be traced back to the 1940s and 1950s in the United States and was first promulgated in a publication in the 1960s. The Reid Technique is mainly used in America and Canada, where evidence obtained by coercive, suggestive, and misleading interviews can be admitted as evidence in the court.

There have been other emerging paradigms in recent years that attempt to further the efficacy of specific aspects of interview outcomes. For example, the Strategic Use of Evidence technique (the SUE technique) is employed to strategically disclose the evidence police are in possession of when interviewing a suspect in order to detect deception (Hartwig, Granhag, Strömwall, & Vrij, 2005; Hartwig, Granhag, Strömwall, & Kronkvist, 2006; Granhag, Strömwall, & Hartwig, 2007). Professors Aldert Vrij (University of Portsmouth, U.K.) and Ronald Fisher (Florida International University, Miami, Florida) lead the work in cognitive measures and verbal cues in detecting lies and deception. The following sections will focus on introducing the PEACE model and the Reid technique, since these two models are by far the most established and utilized models of investigative interviewing.

The PEACE Model

Police forces in Australian states, such as Queensland, Western Australia, and Victoria, utilize the PEACE framework to varying degrees to conduct investigative interviews. The Queensland Police Department has almost entirely incorporated the model into its training manual (Schollum, 2005, p. 44), while Victoria Police use the model primarily for interviews with vulnerable witnesses and has been expanding the training to all detectives (Silvester, 2010).

This interviewing framework is designed for interviews in any situation, with any type of interviewee. Its inception in the United Kingdom in the 1990s was born out of a series of miscarriages of justice and the final quashing of convictions, such as the cases of the Birmingham Six (1974), the Guilford Four (1975), and the Maguire Seven (1976)

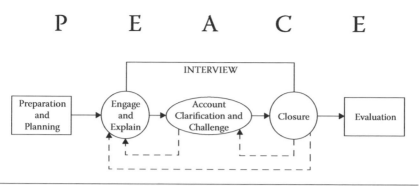

Figure 2.1 The PEACE model is a structure covering interviewing stages.

(Schollum, 2005, p. 23; Gudjonsson, 1992a; Gudjonsson, 2003). Gone are the days when police could begin an interview presuming that the suspect was guilty and they, therefore, could pitch questions that were intimidatory, inflexible, wooden, and biased toward gaining incriminating answers. The spirit of the PEACE model, rather, is to find the truth, whatever it is. The mnemonic PEACE stands for (Schollum, 2005, p. 43) (Figure 2.1):

Planning and Preparation
Engage and Explain
Account
Closure
Evaluation

This interviewing model is a structure covering the before-, during-, and after-interview stages. In the main interviewing stage, as illustrated in the middle part of the diagram in Figure 2.1, there are two different approaches recommended for interviewing witnesses/victims and suspects and uncooperative interviewees, namely cognitive interviewing and conversation management, respectively.

The Cognitive Interview The cognitive interview (CI) was developed by two American psychologists, Ed Geiselman and Ron Fisher, in the 1980s, and was based on empirical research and principles from cognitive and social psychology (Fisher & Castano, 2008, as cited in Holliday, Brainerd, Reyna, & Humphries, 2009, p. 138). It was developed as a means of improving the completeness and accuracy of eyewitness accounts (Geiselman & Fisher, 1985, as quoted in

Schollum 2005, p. 58). Geiselman and Fisher observed hundreds of hours of police interviews recorded on tape and found officers made frequent interruptions, asked too many short-answer questions, and sequenced their questions inappropriately (p. 58). They, therefore, came up with four memory-jogging techniques to be used by police officers in order to elicit the most complete account from cooperative eyewitnesses, namely:

1. Report Everything (RE): To report everything they remembered
2. Reverse Order (RO): To recall events in a variety of chronological orders
3. Change Perspective (CP): To consider the event from someone else's perspective
4. Context Reinstatement (CR): To recall the surrounding physical environment of the incident.

Eyewitnesses are encouraged to close their eyes and imagine they are back at the scene of the crime and to virtually "relive" the event in a cognitive state (Shepherd, 2007, p. 224; Vredeveldt, 2011; Vredeveldt, Hitch, & Baddeley, 2011; Vredeveldt, Baddeley, & Hitch, 2013). The technique also includes forward and backward loops to cover the events before and after the incident, and a reverse memory retrieval technique (Ord, Shaw, & Green, 2011), although the Reverse Order and Change Perspective options have been found to be used less often by police officers (Shepherd, 2007).

Over time, the CI has been modified to cover the entire interview, and is now referred to as the enhanced cognitive interview (ECI). The main stages of ECI (Milne & Bull, 1999, p. 40) include:

Phase 1: Greet and personalize the interview
Establish rapport
Phase 2: Explain the aims of the interview
Phase 3: Initiate a free report

- Context reinstatement
- Open-ended questions
- Pauses
- Nonverbal behavior

Phase 4: Questioning

Phase 5:   Varied and extensive retrieval
Phase 6:   Summary
Phase 7   Closure

Studies conducted on the effectiveness of CI/ECI indicate that these methods elicited more correct information compared with a controlled interview (Gibbons, 2007, p. 146; Gudjonsson, 1992a).

Conversation Management   This method was developed by British psychologist Eric Shepherd to be used on suspects or uncooperative interviewees, requiring free recall, followed by probing and challenges where appropriate (Green, 2011). In conversation management (CM), the interviewer must be more aware of the verbal and nonverbal behaviors of the interviewee, and be aware that the aim of CM is to provide the interviewer with a framework with which to effectively manage the conversation of a reluctant participant. The five stages of CM (Walkley, 1987) are as follows:

1. Contact: Establishing rapport and setting out the aims
2. Content: Eliciting facts using appropriate questioning techniques
3. Conduct: The way in which the content is covered
4. Credibility: The way in which the interviewer is perceived
5. Control: Directing the overall flow of the interview

The Reid Technique

In the United States, the interviewing and interrogation process started to develop in the 1940s and 1950s. Law professor Fred E. Inbau from Northwestern University, and his student John Reid, later founder of John E. Reid & Associates, published the first edition of *Criminal Interrogation and Confessions* (The Williams & Wilkins Company) in 1962. The interviewing techniques promulgated in the book came to be known as the Reid Technique. In the ensuing years, a number of editions were published with further updates and refined techniques; the latest (fifth) edition (Jones & Bartlett Learning) came out in 2011.

The tactics recommended by the book aim to develop police interviewers' skills to persuade a suspect to confess. They include both the interview and interrogation processes. Interviews are nonaccusatory and conducted with a view to gathering information. When criminality is reasonably established, then an interrogation follows and the approaches are accusatory and involve active persuasion. There are three parts to Reid's process (Schollum, 2005, p. 78):

1. Factual analysis of information relative to a crime scene, the victim, and possible subjects: To help determine the direction an investigation should take and offer insights to the possible offender.
2. The interviewing of possible subjects: Using a highly structured interview format that is nonaccusatory and designed to provide the investigator with verbal and nonverbal behavior symptoms that either support probable truthfulness or deception.
3. The accusatory interrogation: Used if the investigator believes that the subject has not told the truth during the nonaccusatory interview.

Reid contends that when an investigator "believes" that the suspect has not told the truth during the nonaccusatory interviewing stage and is "reasonably certain" of the person's guilt, interrogation is then to take place in a controlled environment to seek the truth. There are nine steps in Reid's interrogation technique (Schollum, 2005, p. 78):

Step 1: Positive confrontation
Step 2: Theme development
Step 3: Handling denials
Step 4: Overcoming objections
Step 5: Procurement and retention of a suspect's attention
Step 6: Handling the suspect's passive mood
Step 7: Developing the details of the offense
Step 9: The written confession

Miranda warnings (equivalent to the Police Caution in Australia) must be administered to a custodial suspect and a waiver must be obtained before administering these steps (Buckley, 2006). Kassin and McNall (1991) summarize the two main approaches used by the Reid Technique: maximization (including intimidation, presentation of false evidence, and exaggeration of the seriousness of the crime and the charges) and minimization (including downplaying the seriousness of the crime, offering face-saving excuses, and implying leniency). The technique exerts psychological stress and uncertainty, and it has been criticized for being highly oppressive by forensic psychologists, such as Gisli Gudjonsson (1992a; 1992b; 1999) and Saul Kassin (1997), on the grounds that the technique may lead to false confessions. Moreover, various studies (Gudjonsson & Pearse, 2011; Milne & Bull, 1999; Shepherd, 1988) have found that a lot of accurate information can be elicited in interviews with suspects/witnesses by using less confrontational methods. However, the employment of artifice, trickery, and deception during interrogation still enjoys support from the U.S. public, and is referred to in U.S. literature and supported by the courts. Refer to www.reid.com; Schollum, 2005; Vessel, 1998.

Summary

The authors firmly believe that it is important for interpreters to understand the basic workings of investigative interviewing and the structure of the interviewing model used by the police force they work for. They should be familiar with what questioning procedures apply and how questions are strategically phrased, and which patterns of questions and answers are mostly seen in such interviews. Knowledge in these areas enables interpreters to anticipate better what they must deal with in investigative interviews and to do a better job. The following three chapters will examine common issues and areas of concern encountered in interpreting. Some of these issues also are identified in studies of legal interpreting in court procedures. The chapters will not only outline the areas of concern in general, but also zoom in more specifically on investigative interviews where interpreter intervention can occur and can impact on the interview outcomes.

3

OVERVIEW OF INTERPRETING CHALLENGES AND INTERPRETER CONDUCT ISSUES

Any interpreting event is a communication event that has inherent challenges as we have discussed in the previous chapters. Interpreting as a professional activity needs to meet the quality expectations of clients who rely on this service. Although there is no exhaustive list of all the quality indicators for professional interpreting, the authors have classified interpreting issues under the broad headings of professional conduct issues, linguistic transfer issues. and nonlinguistic issues. The authors approach these topics from the point of view of interpreter intervention and whether an action or utterance by the interpreter is justified or not. The discussions presented in this and the following two chapters have been selected from court interpreting as well as police interview settings, given the close relationship of the two and, particularly, that the police interview is an "upstream event" (Cotterill, 2002, p. 111) in criminal proceedings.

Introduction

This chapter provides an overview of interpreter intervention and then focuses on the issue of professional conduct for interpreters. The other two areas of linguistic transfer issues and nonlinguistic issues will be discussed in the following chapters in detail. The authors propose strategies to minimize unjustified interpreter intervention and highlight those aspects that can be monitored by the interviewer to maintain control and the quality of the interview, when it is conducted via a third party—the interpreter.

Overview of Interpreter Intervention

As we discussed earlier, professional interpreting always takes place in the context of another professional activity. The reason an interpreter is engaged is that the parties in that other professional activity, such as a police interview between a police officer and a suspect or witness, cannot communicate in the language used by the interviewer and need the services of an independent and competent professional interpreter to assist them to communicate. This is essentially what the judge ruled in the murder trial of *Gaio vs. The Queen* (1961), stating that if A and B do not have a common language and, if C is competent in both their languages, then C can act as a conduit between them and interpret what A says to B and what B says to A, and this would be as acceptable as if they had said those words themselves and would not be regarded as hearsay (*Gaio vs. The Queen*, 1961). This decision is one of a few key cases that granted legal status to language interpreting rendered in a court of law. It is significant in that it also defines the parameters within which professional interpreting can take place in legal settings, including police interviews that are often the evidence in a trial.

One measure of the interpreting quality in a bilingual interview can be the assessment of the level of the interpreter's involvement that is beyond what their role is in the interview. It is logical, therefore, to question what role an interpreter plays in such an interview, and the answer is far from straightforward Researchers in the broader legal interpreting field have debated at length about whether the interpreter's role should be active rather than passive, or visible rather than invisible. More discussions on the role of the interpreter are presented in the next section. The interpreter's involvement in a legal setting, including police interviews, is understood to be linguistic mediation between the parties in the communicative event. Broadly speaking, the authors are of the view that the less unjustified intervention there is on the part of the interpreter in the interview, the better the interpreting quality will be. The purpose of this chapter is to discuss some common interpreter conduct issues that may arise in police interpreting (and more generally in legal interpreting), where intervention by the interpreter can be significant, and then to bring these issues to police interviewers' attention so that they feel confident to intervene when the interpreter may act beyond his/her role. Some of these issues were identified in the seminal work of Susan Berk-Selingson (2002) and Sandra Hale (2004) with respect to court interpreting.

The Role of Professional Interpreters

There is much academic debate in the legal interpreting field about what role an interpreter should play in a communicative event where the participants do not speak the same language. On one end of the ledger, metaphors describing interpreters as *"a phono-graph ... a transmission belt ... a bilingual transmitter"* (Morris, 1999, p. 8), an *"electric transformer"* (Wells, 1991, p. 329), or a *"language machine"* (Roberts-Smith, 2009, p. 14), denote the interpreter as "a faceless voice'... in a 'neutral' and nonintrusive way" (Morris, 2010, p. 20), and the interpreter does the job so well that he/she becomes invisible (González, Vasquez, & Mikkelson, 2012).

On the opposite end of the ledger, scholars such as Berk-Seligson (2002) found from her studies that, contrary to the expectations of some judges and attorneys, interpreters are intrusive figures in the courtroom. Consequently, the trials are affected by the interpreters' involvement (ibid). This view is echoed by another American scholar Claudia Angelelli, who opposes the idea that the interpreter should be invisible, contending that such a view "fails to see the interpreter's role for what it really is—that of an individual who orchestrates language, culture, and social factors in a communicative event" (Angelelli, 2004, p. 24).

Other scholars propose different role paradigms to account for different functions interpreters choose to adopt in various interpreted encounters. Swiss researcher Yvan Leanza (2005, pp. 186–187) analyses interpreted medical interviews and suggests that interpreters may adopt four different roles vis-à-vis clients:

1. The role of *system agent* (transmitting the dominant norms, values, and discourse to the patient, ignoring cultural differences).
2. The role of *community agent* (presenting the minority norms and values as potentially equally valid, thus acknowledging cultural differences).

3. The role of *integration agent* (finding resources to facilitate integration by helping migrants and people from the receiving society understand each other, a role that takes place outside medical consultations).

4. The role of *linguistic agent* (attempting to maintain impartiality, intervening only at the language level).

Leading Australian interpreting researcher Professor Sandra Hale (2007) similarly presents five interpreter roles that have either been "openly prescribed" or "deduced" from the performance of interpreters:

1. Advocate for the minority language speaker
2. Advocate for the institution or service provider
3. Gatekeeper (controlling the flow of information from, e.g., lawyer to defendant, by introducing, reinforcing, and excluding topics)
4. Facilitator of communication (feeling responsible for the success of the interaction)
5. Faithful renderer of others' utterances (pp. 101–119)

Coming back to consider the role interpreters play in the legal domain, specifically in a police interviewing setting, the authors of this book are of the view that by taking on any role other than Leanza's "linguistic agent," or Hale's "faithful renderer," interpreters may risk interfering with the overarching relationship between the interviewing police officer and the suspect/witness being interviewed. Although, in real life it may not always be feasible to fully adopt this noninterventionist approach, nonetheless, the authors contend that interpreters should always follow this guiding principle when making decisions. The reason for this position could not be better supported by British psychologist and police trainer Eric Shepherd, who has a designated section in his book *Investigative Interviewing: The Conversation Management Approach* (2007) on the use of interpreters in investigative interviewing, stating that an interpreter "must not act as an intermediary, i.e., must not explain the question to the interviewee nor explain the interviewee's responses" (p. 172). In England and Wales, reregistered Intermediaries come from a range of professional backgrounds, including speech and language therapy, psychology, education, and social work, and they occupy the role of an appropriate adult under paragraph 1.7 of Code C of the Police and Criminal Evidence Act 1984 when the suspect interviewee is either a juvenile or a person who is mentally disordered or mentally vulnerable. This goes to show that "explaining questions to the interviewee" or "explaining the interviewee's responses" (loc. cit.) is a complex matter and it is best left with another appropriately trained professional. Shepherd remarks that "it is certainly the case that many interpreters on their own initiative take on the role of intermediary, and in doing so may make the task of managing the interview very much more difficult" (p. 172).

Conduct Issues of Professional Interpreters

… The interpreter must know from the very first meeting that you [i.e. police interviewer] wish to take active control of the interview even though you do not speak the individual's language.

Shepherd, 2007, p. 173

In a report commissioned by Australia's National Accreditation Authority for Translators and Interpreters, issues relating to professional role and conduct, unfortunately, make up a large part of the complaints about problematic interpreting (Turner & Ozolins, 2007). In *Katsuno et al. v. Australia* (2006) at the UN Human Rights Committee discussed in Chapter 1, five out of the eight interpreting quality issues identified in the case involved problematic roles assumed by the interpreters and inappropriate professional conduct rather than substandard linguistic or transfer skills. We must bear in mind, though, that divergence from the interpreter's appropriate role often features prominently in the discussion of an interpreter's performance and conduct simply because it is easier for the nonbilingual parties to the conversation to detect, whereas linguistic or transfer intervention problems are more difficult to pick up unless there are other bilingual persons present in the conversation or the conversation is recorded and made available for linguistic analysis.

The third of the significant errors listed in the case of *Katsuno et al. v. Australia* (2006) is that the interpreter asked his/her own questions, thinking that he/she was helping the police interviewer. As an example, the following exchange from a courtroom setting between a lawyer and an interpreter illustrates this precise point. (After a long discussion between the interpreter and a witness):

Lawyer: Mr. Interpreter, would you tell us what the witness was saying?
Interpreter: I am trying to get the right answer.

(Order in the Court: The lighter side of the law/the verbatim columns of the Bar news, 1988)

In the previous section, the authors remarked on the risk of interpreters taking on any role other than Leanza's "linguistic agent," or Hale's "faithful renderer." It is because interpreters might, as a result, interfere with the overarching relationship between the interviewing police officer and the suspect/witness when the interviewee may choose to answer questions as much as or as little as they like. The actions interpreters take may change the relationship between the conversing parties in a number of ways, e.g., through providing advice, advocacy, explanation, information, or opinion. In some cases, an interpreter may be taking on the role of the interviewing officer or even another profession, such as the registered intermediary explained above in The Role of Professional Interpreters, without realizing it. British psychologist and police trainer Eric Shepherd recommends that police interviewers conduct a briefing with the interpreter before the start of the interview, setting out their expectations and work rules. Among other points, Shepherd (2007) covers exactly the role and conduct issues we have discussed so far in this chapter. Interpreters should:

- not speak on the suspect's behalf;
- not engage in side conversations with the suspect;
- check if he or she (i.e., the interpreter) is in any doubt as to what is being said by you or the suspect—and let you know about this doubt; and
- not compress or alter whatever is said by you or the suspect.

The contextual and cultural knowledge an interpreter possesses is not there to provide advice on professional or cultural matters either to the interviewing professional or the interviewee. In many countries, the provision of cultural or professional advice in relation to advocacy, migration, welfare, or legal matters is often well regulated and falls within the range of other professions for which there are requirements for minimum training or registration with a professional body. Interpreters should not volunteer cultural or contextual advice and refrain from providing such information when solicited by the unknowing participants of the conversation. Such acts do not fall within their professional role boundaries, and interpreters should feel sufficiently confident to politely ask the party initiating such requests to address the question directly to their conversing counterpart just as they would do to resolve any communication issues in a monolingual conversation. The fifth of the significant errors listed in the case of *Katsuno et al. v. Australia* (2006) concerning the provision of erroneous explanations to the investigator about the social meaning of Japanese terms, highlights the consequences of an interpreter's volunteering of cultural knowledge to the police interviewer. Such errors can and do have serious repercussions in court cases farther down the track. However, it must be pointed out that there may be situations in which an interpreter may need to express an opinion to manage a breakdown in communication. This kind of intervention needs to be clearly identified as the "interpreter's personal opinion" rather than being treated as professional advice born out of the interpreter's responsibility or role, especially in legal settings. Police interviewers must take charge of the interview and attend to any possible breakdown of communication in a bilingual interview just as they would do in a monolingual interview.

Interpreter Giving Instructions or Prodding Speaker Into Action

As is the case in any human interaction, speakers in a conversation, be it monolingual or bilingual, may not understand an instruction or the matter under discussion for a number of reasons, such as ambiguous wording, unusual jargon, hyperformal expressions, or lack of attention. Or, it may simply be that one of the parties chooses to pretend that he/she does not understand for reasons known only to themselves. They may attempt to change the direction of the conversation, they may wish to buy time to formulate a particular response, or they may hold back because they do not want a certain truth to be known as in the following example.

Mr. Justice William Henry Maule (England, 1788–1858) had this exchange with a witness in the Court of Common Pleas:

Witness: You may believe me or not, but I have stated not a word that is false, for I have been wedded to truth from my infancy.

The Court: Yes, sir, but the question is, how long have you been a widower?

(Source: http://www.duhaime.org)

Everyone in the courtroom is entitled to form an opinion on whether the witness is telling the truth, as is clearly expressed by the judge in this exchange. However, it is not the *interpreter's* job to interfere with the witness's statement (had it been an interpreted one) in order to get the truth out for the court or avoid the witness getting himself/herself into trouble. Perhaps a more precise statement should be "everyone *except the interpreter* in the courtroom is entitled to form an opinion" on the witness's credibility. Berk-Selingson (2002) highlights this as an issue in court interpreting.

In the police interview setting, it is not within the interpreter's role to prod the interviewee to answer, redirect the course of the interview to get it "back on the right track" for the interviewing officer, or instruct the interviewee that he/she has not answered the questions asked.

Interpreters must be acutely aware that clarifying instructions or suggesting examples of proper ways of responding are not within their role; rather, this is entirely the prerogative of the professionals. In the case of police interviews, it is the interviewing officer who is in charge of the interview and responsible for what is said and how it is said. If the police officer is not clear, it is up to the suspect/witness to initiate requests for clarification.

Consider the following example.

PO: Do you wish to exercise any of these rights?
Int: xx xxx xxxxxx xxx xxx? (Do you wish to exercise any of these rights?)
S/W: xxx. (Yes)
Int: Yes.
PO: So you understand?
Int: xxxxxx xx xx? (So you understand?)
S/W: Hmmm.
Int: xxx xxxxx xx (Give a verbal yes or no answer).
S/W: xxx (Yes)

In this exchange, the police officer reads the caution before the commencement of the formal interview and asks if the suspect understands that he/she can talk to a lawyer. When the answer to the question: "So you understand?" was an ambiguous "Hmmm," the interpreter intervened by prodding the suspect to give a verbal yes or no answer. The police officer would, at best, notice an extra turn between the interpreter and the interviewee, but, unless he/she asks, would most likely be unaware of the interpreter's having given this instruction to the interviewee. In doing so, the interpreter also limited the choice of answers to either a yes or a no, which would make the suspect believe other possible answers, such as "Not now," "Maybe when I need it," or "Can I have some time to think?" are not acceptable. This was an unjustified intervention by the interpreter and, therefore, is not acceptable as professional interpreting practice.

The following is another example involving a shoplifting suspect:

PO: You had no permission to take that t-shirt from that shop, is that correct?
Int: xxx xx xxxxxx xx xxxxx xxx xxxx xx, xx x?
S/W: (nods)
Int: xxxx xx x xx. (Answer yes or no.)

Giving instructions or prodding the speaker should normally be the role of the professional who is conducting the interview. Unjustified intervention by the interpreter may pressure the witness/suspect into a premature answer when he/she does not understand the question clearly or wishes to supply an alternative response that has not been offered in the question.

One of the ways the interpreter can manage such situations (e.g., when getting body language instead of a verbal response as an answer) is to tell the police officer, in audio taped interviews, that the answer was not verbalized, so the police officer can decide how to handle it. Another way to manage the situation would be for the interpreter to say, "The speaker nodded yes" or "The speaker nodded no." The police officer can then decide whether indicating a response by nodding is acceptable or not, especially when the interview is to be presented to the court as evidence, and especially when in some cultures shaking the head means yes and nodding means no.

Managing Issues Resulting From Power Asymmetry

Interpreters possess a certain level of power precisely because two people who do not share a common language depend on the interpreter's service to communicate. Interpreters also acquire confidential information about the parties during an assignment. This means the persons who rely on the interpreter are vulnerable to some extent. Professional interpreters working in police and court settings must be aware that they cannot serve one party more than the other. This is sometimes the only reason a professional, impartial interpreter is called for by one or both parties. Failing to act for each client impartially and equally would be a breach of the trust both parties have in the interpreter. Serving one party more than the other can consist of giving advice, hiding information, or misinterpreting utterances on purpose in order to help one party achieve their objectives. Parties to an interview may ask interpreters for advice or assistance, hoping that the interpreter's unique position may help them to improve their own situation. Professional interpreters must refrain from responding to such requests. One way to manage this can be to advise the parties before an interview that everything they say will be interpreted to the other party (including any requests or demands) and if they wish something not to be interpreted, they should not say it at all.

Summary

This chapter highlights that interpreting is one of the few professions that take place entirely within another professional activity. This distinguishing characteristic of professional interpreting must be fully appreciated by interpreters, as well as the clients they are interpreting for, as it draws the parameters within which interpreters can move. The yardstick to evaluate quality of interpreting performance, particularly in a high-stakes police interviewing setting, is to determine if they move within their role of linguistic facilitation competently and allow the police interviewer and the suspect or witness interviewee to communicate as closely as possible to an interview, which has no language barrier.

4

LINGUISTIC TRANSFER ISSUES IN POLICE INTERPRETING AND RECOMMENDED STRATEGIES

Professional interpreters must possess a high level of competence in the languages in which they work. The level of competency required has been discussed in Chapter 1 under the subheading of Skills Required for Interpreting (see p. 11). In the context of police and legal procedures, this means that a professional interpreter needs to be competent in everyday language as well as being familiar with specialist vocabulary and registers specific to police and legal processes and procedures in both languages.

Introduction

As discussed earlier in Chapter 1 under the subheading of The Interpreting Process (see p. 3), the main focus in any interpreted event is to convey meaning from one language into another in order to enable parties involved to communicate. In police and legal contexts, however, this approach needs to be applied with great care. The main reason for this is that oral or written evidence obtained from a suspect or witness in an interpreted interview is often subject to detailed scrutiny later on in the legal process, and what is actually said by one party and what is actually meant can be a point of dispute. A fully meaning-based approach may face a great number of challenges or claims of inaccuracies, justified or unjustified, during the legal process, e.g., during cross-examination in a hearing.

A seemingly simple word, sentence, or a short utterance, may have a number of interpretations, depending on the context. In this respect, a police officer or a lawyer may pursue a number of alternatives. The interpreter, on the other hand, is placed in the difficult situation of being forced to choose only one, instantly, and to be held accountable for that choice.

This is where a literal approach to interpreting (and translating, for that matter,) in police and, in general legal settings, may need to be adopted as much as the linguistic resources of the target language permit. For example, calling someone a "bear" is very offensive in Turkish culture, whereas in English, it is not. An English speaker would probably express the same feelings using another animal, such as a "pig." The dilemma for the interpreter in a police interpreting setting lies in whether the interpreter should literally say "bear" in English and allow the parties to prove it is offensive, or whether the interpreter should adopt a communicative approach and say "pig," for example, to at least convey the offensive nature of the use of the word "bear" to someone who otherwise would not know. We argue that in legal settings where even the meaning of the wording in legislation is argued in lengthy legal debates, an interpreter's choice of the word "pig" may be very difficult to defend as it includes the interpreter's personal interpretation of the word "bear." What "bear" is intended to mean by the interviewee should be left for the interviewer to clarify through further questioning.

A similar issue may arise in cases where a suspect or witness says or does something and an interpreter further adds to what they have said or done by verbalizing it more specifically. For example, if a victim, answering a question about where he feels the pain most has occurred as a result of a physical assault, responds "here" (pointing to his lower back) or simply points with no verbal response, an interpreter who has a clear view of the area being pointed to may be tempted to say "lower back," intending a meaning or communicative-based approach. The victim, in fact, may have meant to say "lower back," and, if it were during a medical consultation, the interpreter's handling of this by saying "lower back" would probably be acceptable. However, in a police interview, where what is said and how it is said may be subject to scrutiny in a later trial, the interpreter's handling may be challenged, as the victim does not specify "lower back," but simply points and says "here."

Style of Interpreting: Free versus Literal

In the broader field of translating and interpreting studies, there has been endless debate on which approach should be adopted for which kind of text/discourse. An imaginary continuum with a strictly literal (word-for-word) approach and a completely free (sense-for-sense) approach sitting on the two ends serves to accommodate various schools of thought and justification. In the field of legal and police interpreting, on the one hand, there is the legal professionals' perennial request for interpreters to "not interpret, just translate everything literally," placing the kind of interpretation they prefer to go toward the more literal end of the continuum. On the other hand, U.S. interpreting practitioner and educator Holly Mikkelson (1999) encourages interpreters not to be afraid "to use common sense and good judgment in determining how to render the language of the courtroom … in an efficient and intelligible manner, while retaining all elements of meaning and style," allowing interpreters more leeway in the process of language transfer. This middle-ground view notes that "the form and style of the message are regarded as equally important elements of meaning" in courtroom discourse, and that interpreters must mediate between the verbatim requirement of the legal record and the need to convey a meaningful message in the target language (TL).

Mikkelson and colleagues suggest that interpreters should focus on conceptual units that must be conserved, not word-by-word, but concept-by-concept. In other words, they have to be true to the global source language (SL) message, but also take pains to conserve paralinguistic elements, such as hesitations, false starts, hedges, and repetitions in a verbatim style and insert them in the corresponding points of the TL (González, Vásquez, & Mikkelson, 1991, pp. 16–17).

The authors of this book have adopted a practical approach to this age-old debate. We would argue that the debate must take into account the rules and guidelines other professions have about how things can be and should be said due to the fact that interpreting takes place within another professional activity and, by default, interpreters are bound by the rules and guidelines of that professional setting, which may not always leave interpreters the discretion of choosing an interpreting approach or style at their will. This is nowhere more so than in the legal field.

The Law and Words

Law is about the interpretation of words, and lengthy legal debates over what is actually meant by a specific word uttered by someone are not just confined to law and order programs on TV, but take place every day in courts at all levels. The issue of word meaning in mono-lingual settings must be highlighted as it has significant implications for interpreters. The lexical choices interpreters make during a police interview will be subject, sometimes almost instantaneously, to close scrutiny by the interviewing police officer, and may, at later trials, give rise to hours of examination of and debate over the interpretation of the TL words rendered by the interpreter.

A review of the literature identifies three common approaches to how words are interpreted (in the monolingual sense) in law. These include a literal approach, a purpose focused approach, and a mischief approach (Chisholm, 2007). This is not so dissimilar to the age-old debate in the interpreting/translating field as to whether interpreting should be performed literally, or otherwise, depending on either its Skopos (purpose), or based on its communicative intent. The three approaches to "interpreting" the word of the law are explained below.

Literal Rule

The literal rule of statutory interpretation refers to accepting the ordi-nary and natural meaning of words, if there is a dispute about what is meant in a particular piece of legislation.

Example:
R vs. Harris (1836) 7 C & P 446

The defendant bit off his victim's nose. The offense in the statute read: "It is an offense to stab, cut, or wound" someone. The defendant argued "he did not stab, cut, or wound." The court held that, when lit-erally interpreted, the act of biting did not come within the meaning of stab, cut, or wound as these words implied an instrument had to be used. Therefore, the defendant's conviction was quashed.

Source: e-lawresources.co.uk

Purpose (Golden) Rule

Interpreting legislation also may be guided by the purpose of the legislation if a literal approach produces absurd results. This is called the "purposive approach." Australia's Interpretation Act 1984 (WA) Sect 18 (AUSLII (c)) favors this approach. As a result, if there is an ambiguous word or expression in the legislation, the reader has to try to work out what its purpose or object is, and interpret its meaning accordingly in a particular context.

Example:
Adler vs. George (1964) 2 QB 7

Under the Official Secrets Act 1920, it was an offense to obstruct a member of the armed forces "in the vicinity" of a prohibited place. The defendant claimed he was not in the *vicinity* of it, but was actually *in* the prohibited place and, therefore, did not commit the offense. The court applied the golden (purpose) rule. It would be absurd for a person to be liable if they were near to a prohibited place and not if they were actually in it. His conviction, therefore, was upheld.

Source: e-lawresources.co.uk

Mischief Rule

The mischief rule allows a court to look at what "mischief" or problem the statute was originally seeking to rectify and interpret a word in consideration of this (Chisholm, 2007).

Example:
Elliot vs. Grey (1960) 1 QB 367

The defendant's car was parked on the road. It was jacked up and had its battery removed. He was charged with an offense under the Road Traffic Act 1930 of using an uninsured vehicle on the road. The defendant argued he was not *"using"* the car on the road as clearly it was not drivable and, therefore, he did not commit an offense.

The statute was aimed at ensuring people were compensated when injured due to the hazards created by others. The court applied the mischief rule and held that the car was being used on the road as it represented a hazard and, therefore, insurance would be required in the event of an incident. He was convicted.

Source: e-lawresources.co.uk

One of the most significant implications of legal interpretation (in the monolingual sense) of words for language interpreters is that it limits the options available for interpreters in transferring meaning between languages. A totally free, idiomatic approach to interpreting, however natural it may sound and no matter how well it may serve the purpose in many other settings, may be attacked by a defendant's legal team in a later trial and, in fact, may lead to the collapse of a case. This means the choice to interpret freely or literally or anything in between is not something that is solely decided by the interpreter. Interpreters need to be aware of, and respect, how words are treated in the context in which they work.

The Power of Words

Linguistic choices have been proven to influence both participants in the communicative event and the intended audience of that communication. The wording in a question may lead to different answers although the question is about the same thing. Questions, such as: "How dangerous is this game?" or "How safe is this game?," may elicit different answers, although the questions refer to exactly the same game.

Examples of words being used to influence the speakers or the audience can be found in public service leaflets, statements made by politicians, commercials, and advertisements. For example, in the heated public debate on euthanasia, those who advocate euthanasia will say "ending someone's suffering," whereas those who are against euthanasia will say "killing someone." Words are carefully chosen to convey a particular attitude to the readers or the audience, and interpreters (and translators) must develop sensitivity toward the differences in meaning various words convey in order to be able to render them accurately.

An interpreter working in a police or legal setting is expected by the parties involved to produce in the other language not just what is said but also how it is said. This presents challenges to a meaning-based approach to interpreting, as interpreters would be less able to use strategies, such as paraphrasing or cultural substitution, which may be acceptable in other settings. Obviously there will be occasions where the exact reproduction of what and how something is said into another language is unachievable simply because linguistic differences do not allow it. However, interpreters should be aware of these aspects of linguistic transfer and should attempt to reproduce them as closely to the SL as possible in the TL, especially in a legal and police interviewing context. Interpreters may need to use the meaning-based approach as an alternative strategy where the result produced by a literal interpretation is absurd or meaningless in a particular context. They, however, should be prepared to justify their lexical choices or other strategies they have used. So, if we revisit the example given earlier at the start of this chapter about calling someone a "bear" in Turkish, the interpreter has to be prepared to justify why he/she interpreted the Turkish word "bear" as "pig" in English when and if this particular rendition is called into question, say, in a court or police interpreting setting. The justification may be that the context within which the term "bear" is used in the SL is completely unambiguous, and, therefore, the choice of "pig" in the TL is appropriate. Or, if the interpreter decides to leave the term "bear" literally in the TL, there may be subsequent enquiries from the lawyers in the court or the interviewing officer in the police interview about the intended meaning of the word "bear" in this context. The interpreter can then convey the question back to the interviewee who used the expression and eventually the original intention to use it as a derogatory term in the SL will be ferreted out.

Handling Interviewer's Rapport-Building Strategies

Rapport-building has received significant attention as an effective interview strategy, and it is sanctioned as an important step in the enhanced version of the Cognitive Interview as discussed in Chapter 2.

Communicating empathy is a guiding principle in attempts to build rapport (Rogers, 1942, as cited in Milne & Bull, 1999). This can be done in a number of ways, both verbally and through nonverbal acts, such as nodding your head in agreement.

The interviewer may follow a deliberate discursive style to build rapport with the interviewee, e.g., by choice of grammatical structures, lexical items, or other linguistic or paralinguistic features. The speaker's deliberate choice of a particular discursive feature needs to be identified and maintained by the interpreter. Neuroscientists, such as O'Connor and Seymour (1990), approach rapport-building using a neurolinguistic programming theory. They assert that individuals store information using one dominant sense, such as vision (visual-dominant), hearing (auditory-dominant), or touch (kinesis-dominant) over others. If an interviewer can identify the dominant sense of the interviewee, this would assist in rapport building; communication differences can be minimized and more information is likely to be collected. The preferred sense can be an individual feature or can be a cultural choice. Some cultures may tend to express information using a particular sense.

Interviewing researchers and practitioners Lord and Cowen (2011, p. 85) provide the following examples of how the choice of dominant sense may impact on the interviewer's choice of words or construction of questions. An interviewer may say: "Try to look back and see if you can recall," when the interviewee is visual-dominant, or "Does it ring a bell?" for auditory-dominant subjects. In the case of a kinesis-dominant subject, "How did you feel when you saw this happen? How do you think they felt?' may be preferred. Lord and Cowen propose that it is most constructive to begin a conversation with the sense with which the witness associates. This helps the witness to become comfortable and more cooperative.

Whether the interpreter agrees or not with the efficacy of these proposed interviewing techniques, if such wording is used in an inter-preted interview, these discursive features deliberately produced by the interviewer need to be reproduced in the other language by the interpreter. Otherwise, it may potentially interfere with the rapport building attempt intended by the interviewer. This would be difficult for the interpreter to justify.

Active listening is another form of maintaining rapport with an interviewee. One of the ways active listening can be demonstrated is through the use of mirror key word repetition.

Milne and Bull (1999) offered the following example:

S/W: "A man just burst into the shop *with a gun.*"
PO: "*With a gun.* Did he then talk to anyone?"

(Italics added)

If this takes place in an interpreted interview, the interpreter needs to pay close attention to reproducing the interviewer's attempt to mirror the interviewee. As we know, occasionally interpreters, under pressure to maintain the flow of communication, may decide it is more important to interpret the new utterance: "Did he then talk to anyone?" and drop the repeated utterance "with a gun." An interpreter with specialist training would pick this up and try to produce these deliberate utterances as precisely as possible in the other language and be careful not to interfere with the interviewer's set objectives.

Misinterpreting Lexical Items/Collocations

Misinterpreting lexical items or collocations (the co-occurrence of words) is an area that receives a lot of attention, if not most of the attention, in any examination of interpreting quality. It is not surprising that the first and the last points in the list of significant interpreting errors in *Katsuno et al. v. Australia* (2006) discussed in Chapter 1 has to do with misinterpreting of lexical items. Often people will raise questions about the accuracy of the lexical choices made by an interpreter. While criticism of this nature sometimes actually relates to stylistic issues, nevertheless, such an error is still referred to as an issue of using the "wrong word." The misinterpreting of lexical items is most obvious and serious if it occurs at the level of propositional meaning, i.e., the primary meaning of a word.

Let us return to the example from Chapter 2 (Lexical Choice), where the BBC News (April 13, 2012) reported a trial being aborted and a retrial ordered because an interpreter (interpreting in a police interview) confused the word "beaten" with "bitten." When one of the defendants was later questioned, in cross examination, to show where he was bitten, he said he had never said "bitten" and he, in fact, had said "beaten." This may or may not be a comprehension issue, or it might be a pronunciation issue that resulted in inaccurate transcription. Nonetheless, it shows how interpreting errors at the level of primary meaning can have serious consequences in legal and police interviewing settings.

Consider the following example, which includes a misinterpretation of a lexical item in a police interview.

PO: Have you *had any contact* with your ex-wife recently?
INT: xxxx xxx xxxx xx xxx xxx xxx x xxx xx xx xxx?* (Have you *talked* to your ex-wife recently?)
S/W: No.

(Note: But he, in fact, sent his ex-wife text messages>)

The misinterpretation of the propositional meaning of the lexical item "contact" distorts its primary meaning and cannot be justified by the interpreter. Such an error is significant as it leads the interviewer to think the suspect is lying because the interviewer knows from the wife's statement to the police that the suspect had sent his ex-wife text messages. The suspect answered correctly by saying "no" to the question: "Have you talked to your wife recently?" as he had not talked to his wife, but is misled by the interpretation because the meaning of the lexical item "contact" was incorrectly conveyed.

Misinterpreting the propositional meaning of lexical items is an indicator of poor-quality interpreting. It often results from the interpreter's lack of precise comprehension of the meaning rather than from a poor choice of equivalent in the other language. On the other hand, propositional meaning is the level where most languages have more in common and where finding an equivalent meaning in the target language can be easier compared with figurative or connotational meaning. For this reason, interviewing officers may try to word their questions using words in their primary meanings, as a strategy to minimize occurrences of misinterpreted/misunderstood lexical items in interpreted interviews. For instance, instead of asking: "What *was running through your mind* when you saw the riots?" an interviewing officer might ask: "What *were you thinking* (or *what were you feeling*) when you saw the riots?" This should minimize the chance that the interpreter might focus on a word, such as "running," and try to translate it literally, rather than recognizing it as a figure of speech.

However, the more experienced and competent interpreters are, the better they should be able to handle figurative and metaphorical expressions, connotational meanings, and so on. Nevertheless, even with an experienced and highly skilled interpreter, choosing words used in their primary or literal meanings as much as possible will help to reduce the cognitive demand on the interpreter. In the area of aerospace, automotive, healthcare, semiconductors, and telecommunications, where English is used as the common language for worldwide communication, there has been continual development and implementation since the 1970s of "controlled English" to "enhance the readability, comprehensibility, and usability of a text for global readers" (Quah, 2006, p. 49) by limiting the size of vocabulary, the level of complexity of phrases and sentences, and the style of discourse (ibid). Kaji (1999) at Japanese Hitachi's Central Research Laboratory defines a "controlled language" to be "a subset of a natural language with artificially restricted vocabulary, grammar, and style" (p. 37). By applying the principles of a controlled language in the above-mentioned industries, highly homogenous and easily understood TL in multilingual translation tasks have become achievable, using "simple vocabulary and sentence structure in order to convey complex ideas in writing to ensure rapid reading, understanding, and ease of translation" (Quah, 2006, p. 48). It may be worth considering developing detailed police questioning protocols applying the controlled language principles in order to minimize incidents of "lost in translation" and give interviewing officers more control in interviews where they have to rely on interpreters.

Misinterpreting Grammatical Structures/Units

Grammatical structures/units, e.g., number, gender, tense, aspect, voice, also convey significant elements of meaning. Failing to convey meaning expressed through grammatical structures in police/legal interpreting can also have serious consequences and implications as much as misinterpreting a lexical item such as a word or a phrase, with which interpreters tend to be more preoccupied.

Example:

"Did you see the man striking the woman?"

versus

"Did you see the man strike the woman?" (Magliano, 2014)

The aspect in the first sentence that indicates non-completion of the action of 'hitting' would be lost if it is interpreted as in the second sentence, which indicates action was completed or was a one-time event.

Active and Passive Sentence Structures

The use of active and passive structures may differ from one language to another. Some languages encourage the use of active structures as they sound more natural and friendly, whereas some other languages may prefer passive sentence structures because they may be regarded as more formal and learned. This has been identified as an issue by Berk-Selingson (2002) in court interpreting.

In police interpreting, and in legal interpreting in general, active and passive structure shifts need to be handled carefully. Examples below show how the focus shifts away from the suspect to the agent of the action, or vice versa, when the structure shifts from passive to active.

Were you contacted?
Did they contact you?

or

I was included.
They included me.

or

Were you cautioned by the police officer?
Did the police officer give you a caution?

or

Were you allowed to contact your relatives by the police officer?
Did the police officer allow you to contact your relatives?

When interpreting into the TL, interpreters may inadvertently switch from active structures to passive structures, or vice versa, as one structure may be more common or acceptable than the other in the other language. Given the fact that active or passive structures may influence speakers or third party audiences, such as juries or judges, interpreters must be sensitized to these structures and handle them with care when transferring them into the TL. Interpreters should not assume that lexical equivalence has the greatest priority when they undertake their work and make the mistake of relegating other linguistic aspects, such as grammatical structures, to secondary consideration.

Definite and Indefinite Articles

According to the World Atlas of Language Structures Online (http://wals.info/feature/37A#2/25.5/148.2), 198 languages in the world have no definite or indefinite article, and 45 have no definite article, only indefinite articles. When interpreting from languages that have no definite and/or indefinite articles into English, interpreters need to be careful in extracting the information from the context, or take the initiative to clarify whether an indefinite article (such as "a boy" to denote new information) or a definite article (such as "the boy" to denote known information) should be used. Failure to do so may have serious legal implications, such as the case involving the Korean language reported by interpreting researcher Jieun Lee (2009, pp. 390–394) in a New South Wales local court.

The defendant in the case maintained that when he brought a packet of condoms along with noodles and drinks in a plastic bag to the hotel room, the complainant may have seen the condom packet when she took out the noodles. However, the complainant maintained that she did not take the noodles from the bag, and therefore, had no knowledge about the condoms. She went to the police station and made a complaint to the police about the defendant, and then made a phone call at the police station that was recorded by the police without the knowledge of the defendant. The Korean conversation was subsequently transcribed and translated as follows:

1 Complainant: ... I just don't understand. I want to know the reason. Did you have the condom?
2 Complainant: Hello?
3 Defendant: Yeah ...
4 Complainant: Did you have the condom on?

NOISE ...

5 Complainant: Uh?
6 Defendant: It was ... on that day ...
7 Complainant: What? I asked you whether you had condom on, on that day?
8 Defendant: On that day?

Lee suggests that the zero determiner in turn 7 for the previously mentioned "condom" in turns 1 and 4 is "either a grammatical mistake by the translator or an indication that the translator could not identify a determiner in translating the utterance in turn 7" (ibid, p. 392). This issue was later exploited by the defense lawyer as an attack on the complainant's credibility:

> ... *the condom is of significant proportions in this case ... she says that she didn't see any condoms there that night. I suggest TO you by the very words she used to Richard [the defendant] himself. She's telling lies and she tripped herself UP because she's probably forgotten what she said to Richard on the phone ... not a condom. THE condom. The definite article. She could only*

have been talking … of the CONDOM which she would've KNOWN about back on … March 200* [SIC] and she did in FACT see the condom packet … but the fact of the matter is, she was aware that there was a condom because she SAID in her conversation with HIM: "did you have the condom on."

This goes to show, on the one hand, how important it is to note any ambiguity when an interpreter is called upon to do telephone transcription and translation. On the other hand, had such a conversation happened in a face-to-face police interpreting setting, we could now see how critical it is for the interpreter to clarify ambiguities in meaning in the other language so the appropriate definite/indefinite articles can be used in the English rendition.

Personality and Linguistic Skills: Author Profiling

Through the linguistic and extralinguistic features of the way they speak, people reveal information, such as their educational background, upbringing, social attitudes, and personalities. It can be grammatical structures, phrases, collocations, and lexical choices that provide the clues. It also can be the accent, pronunciation, and the demeanor that reveal the signs. In the same way, a suspect or witness's utterances may be significant for some aspect of the investigation, for example, whether two threatening messages were written by the same person. The interviewee's linguistic reactions and style of speech, if not conveyed adequately by the interpreter, may be misleading or, at worst, may hamper the investigation.

The interviewee's style of speech and idiosyncrasies may include, for example, use of a particular word or words. It may contribute to the identification of an author/speaker or provide clues about his/her background. It may be possible to say that a person is unlikely to know a word that occurs in a language sample and, therefore, is unlikely to be the author of that sample. Or there may be technical or specialized vocabulary that a person is unlikely to know, or, in the case of a second language speaker, words beyond his/her current level of development (Gibbons, 2007). A lexical item or a particular usage may indicate that the person is a speaker from a particular region or country where the language is spoken and this information may be significant in a police investigation.

Interpreters must handle with care these aspects of speech, as they have significant implications in the police/legal context. The interpreter's bilingual competence should be at an advanced level in order to identify, preserve, and express the features whenever and wherever it is linguistically possible. A less competent or untrained interpreter may not be sensitive enough to pick up the linguistic and extralinguistic features, or may suppress, distort, or omit them altogether.

Managing Speech Styles of Speakers

One other discourse feature to be managed by interpreters is the speech style of the speaker. This can be narrative style (used by someone who gives long answers to questions) or fragmented style (used by someone who answers in a brief, concise manner) as in the following examples (O'Barr, 1982, p. 76):

Narrative Speech Style:

Q: Now, calling your attention to the twenty-first day of November, a Saturday, what were your working hours that day?

A: Well, I was working from, uh, 7 a.m. to 3 p.m. I arrived at the store at 6:30 and opened the store at 7.

Fragmented Speech Style

Q: Now, calling your attention to the twenty-first day of November, a Saturday, what were your working hours that day?

A: Well, I was working from 7 to 3.

Q: Was that 7 a.m.?

A: Yes.

Q: And what time that day did you arrive at the store?

A: 6:30.

Q: 6:30. And did, uh, you open the store at 7 o'clock?

A: Yes, it has to be opened by then.

In the well-publicized O. J. Simpson case in California, the defense lawyer demonstrated that a witness lacked credibility by citing parts of this witness's previous official narrative, and confronting him with his present fragmented version of the facts. The style of the speaker may have significance for the interviewers, as well as later on, in the courtroom for the judges and jury. People project their images (e.g., friendliness, credibility, social status, etc.) in the social context through the language they use. By the same token, we can all relate to how we judge someone to be, for example, truthful, knowledgeable, or snobbish by what they say and how they say things. It is no wonder speech styles have been the subject of research in the social psychology of language.

U.S. linguist Robin Lakoff's 1975 publication *Language and Woman's Place* pioneered the analysis of language attributes that are associated with powerful and powerless social images. Based on Lakoff's (1975) seminal work, the following are considered to manifest powerless speech style:

- Hedges: sort of, kind of, you know
- Hesitation: um, er, oh well, let's see
- Uncertainty: often asking questions
- Use of sir/ma'am
- Intensifiers: very, definitely, surely
- Taking longer time to say the same thing

(Gibbons, 2007)

- (Super) polite forms, e.g., I'd really appreciate if …
- Tag questions, e.g., John is here, isn't he?
- Speaking in italics, e.g., so or very (intonation)
- Empty adjectives, e.g., divine, charming, cute, sweet
- Direct quotations, e.g., quoting directly instead of paraphrasing

(O'Barr, 1982, p. 63)

Leaving aside the gender debate sparked by Lakoff's attributing the speech style of women to their "powerlessness" and the relationship between language and gender, the powerful versus powerless speech styles proposed by Lakoff (1975a) have far-reaching implications in the legal sphere where accounts by suspects and witnesses are subject to scrutiny by others both on the content of their accounts and the way they express themselves.

In the 1970s to early 1980s, U.S. sociology and English professor William O'Barr (1982, p. 74) conducted experiments on close to 100 university students as mock jurors using a 15-minute scripted courtroom testimony as the research tool. He incorporated various linguistic features into the same script and made it into two versions of the same courtroom discourse: one in powerful speech style and the other powerless. The research outcome indicated that the mock jurors regarded the testimony significantly more positively when it was rendered using the powerful speech style. They said the version is more:

- Convincing
- Truthful
- Competent
- Intelligent
- Trustworthy

Professional interpreters working in court and police settings should take particular heed of O'Barr's research findings in that speech styles change people's perception of one's self projection and it must be re-expressed by interpreters in a bilingual setting in order to minimize unjustified intervention on the interpreter's part. Interpreters must sensitize themselves on the above powerless speech attributes and practice rendering them in the languages in which they work.

Summary

Interpreting involves at least two languages. Given the differences between languages, it is understandable that a basic principle of interpreting is to try to transfer meaning, not individual words. In police and legal contexts, however, the oral or written evidence obtained from a suspect or witness in an interpreted interview is often subject to detailed scrutiny later on in the legal process. A fully meaning-based approach, without regard to *how* the utterance is said and to the words chosen to express the meaning, might be exposed to legal challenges during the legal process.

5

OTHER LINGUISTIC RELATED AND NONLINGUISTIC ISSUES IN POLICE INTERPRETING AND RECOMMENDED STRATEGIES

Interpreting is often regarded by lay people as a simple linguistic conversion by which words in one language are replaced with words in another language. We have argued throughout this book why this is not so. Linguistic transfer skills, whether these involve replacing words with other words or using other strategies, such as paraphrasing, substituting, using more general/more specific terms, etc., address only part of the interpreter's exercise in transferring meaning accurately from one language to another. A number of nonlinguistic factors also can have a significant impact on the interpreting process and the quality of its outcome.

Introduction

An interpreter has to handle many interpersonal factors (Dean & Pollard, 2001) that may arise when dealing with, for example, difficult clients, distressed witnesses, or overworked police officers. The interpreter also must be able to identify and resolve any environmental factors (ibid) that may affect interpreting quality (e.g., when the venue lacks privacy or is too noisy or too hot/cold). Furthermore, the interpreter has to monitor and coordinate the flow of communication between the conversing parties (e.g., when overlapping of talk prevents effective interpreting or a party talks for too long without a pause for interpreting). And, finally, there are the intrapersonal factors (ibid) that affect the interpreting situation, for example, if the interpreter feels emotionally drained by a victim's account or is physically unwell for some reason.

As with all other professions, professional interpreters must culti-
vate the ability to reflect in action (while interpreting) and reflect on
action (after completing the assignment). Education theorist Donald
Schön (1983) regards the capacity for professionals to "think what they
are doing while they are doing it" as a key skill. He asserts that the only
way to manage the "indeterminate zones of [professional] practice" is
through the ability to think on your feet, and apply previous experience
to new situations. The authors of this book are of the view that professional interpreters must develop linguistic and nonlinguistic competencies in order to analyze challenges arising from real-life interpreting
assignments, which are not limited to linguistic problems, and assess
the strategies to address them and make the choice of the best option
for the situation—all in a split second. This is where the accumulation of experience, briefing and debriefing with the professional, and
seeking mentorship from senior colleagues become valuable. In the
police setting, police briefing of interpreters prior to interviews on such
things as the technique to be employed, potential challenges, expectations, and how to solve problems that may arise, can help in addressing
some of these issues in order to achieve better interviews.

Managing Turn-Taking

In any dialogue or conversation, including interviews, the parties need
to take turns speaking. The timing of the changing of turns is determined firstly by the linguistic content, e.g., through the completion
of a syntactic unit; secondly, by the paralinguistic features, e.g., fall-
ing or rising tone, slowing of speech, or complete silence; and lastly,
by body language, such as eye contact or gestures (Paltridge, 2006,
p. 113). In most conversations, turn-taking happens naturally and
smoothly, and the parties follow the "unspoken" turn-taking rules
to achieve the aim of the communication. In interpreted interviews,
however, the turn-taking pattern gets complicated in the sense that
the interpreter needs to have a turn before the next speaker gets the
turn. In most cases it works without any problems because the parties
quickly pick up the pattern and wait for the interpreter to finish the
interpretation of the previous turn. The most common way of telling it
is time for a change of turn in a monolingual setting is when the other
party pauses, uses rising/falling intonation, interrupts by starting to

talk, or simply raises his/her hand to indicate a stop. In conversations or interviews where the purpose is to elicit information, turn-taking may be strategically applied by parties to their own ends.

Example:

PO: What sort of connection do you have to the shop?
S/W: Nothin (short pause) … Betty and I we've … Aw, we've been together for nine years de facto relationship. We …
PO: W'l who's Betty?

(Heydon, 2005. p. 101)

In this example, the suspect pauses after saying "nothin" and since the police officer chooses not to take the turn, the suspect then decides to continue, revealing further information about another person involved, "Betty," and the police officer then follows up this new information, which came about through voluntary disclosure by the suspect. If this had been interpreted, the interpreter would have needed to manage this carefully. If the interpreter started interpreting during the pause after "*nothin,*" the turn would probably go back to the police officer, who would then ask another question.

Consider another example below:

PO: The cab driver says you were *yelling at him.*
S/W: xxx, x xxx xxx xx xxx (*****) xxx xx xxx xxxx xxx xx.*
(Yes, I was yelling at him(*****) but only after he slammed the door in my face.)

If the interpreter decides to interrupt the witness at the point indicated by (*****) because he/she thinks that the suspect is catching his breath and has already answered the question, it is highly likely that the next turn will be taken over by the police officer, who may be satisfied by the answer and continue with another question. In such cases, the explanation may never be forthcoming as the police officer or the suspect would not be able to pick this up.

Interpreters need to be aware of this sort of premature intervention in turn-taking and try to let the speaker complete what they would like to say, to the extent that the interpreter's short-term memory capacity allows. Furthermore, a pause may be placed deliberately by the interviewer for a purpose, e.g., to provoke the suspect. In such a situation, if an interpreter commences interpreting as soon as a pause occurs, it may defeat the purpose of the pause or interrupt prematurely what the person originally intended to say, thus preventing, perhaps, the revelation of information that may be important. One way of minimizing this risk is, if the parties are seated in a three-cornered arrangement (common in Australia where police interviews are video recorded and all parties need visual contact for nonverbal cues and for line of sight in sign language interpreting), when the interpreter finishes interpreting, he/she can physically turn toward or make eye contact with the speaker who was interrupted to indicate that they may continue to finish what they were saying. If an interpreter is seated behind the interviewee (as is recommended in some countries), this can be indicated verbally. Such measures can help maintain the natural order of turns as they would have been had this been a monolingual dialogue. Professionals, such as police officers, also can keep an eye on this aspect and may need to remind the interviewee that they want them to continue telling his/her story from where the interpreter interrupted.

Another issue that comes up with managing turns is when one of the parties repeats a question or utterance to the other speaker in order to confirm or verify what was said. The interpreter sometimes intuitively responds with the information known to him/her from the previous exchanges.

Example:

PO: What time did you last see the shop owner?
INT: xxxx xxxx xx xxx xxx xxx xxxx?
S/W: Uhm ... xx xxx xxx xxx xx. (Uhm ... it was about half past nine.)
INT: It was about half past nine.
PO: Half past nine?
INT: Nine thirty.

In this example, the interpreter, not the suspect, confirms the time, as the interpreter fails to pass the turn back to the suspect by answering the question posed by the police officer directly. This is quite common in interpreted interviews and often looks like a harmless facilitation of communication or even a time-saving measure. However, it may have significant implications for evidence in criminal cases, when scrutinized in later court proceedings. Interpreters should avoid answering questions on behalf of the interviewee, even if the answer may be clear from the exchanges so far. The police officer may have asked the question: "Half past nine?" for several reasons: to check if he/she has understood the time correctly or to try to ascertain how the suspect knew the time (e.g., was it a guess or did the suspect happen to check the time to catch a bus). Interviewing officers should monitor the interpreter's rendition carefully and bring to the interpreter's attention that they want the answer to be provided by the interviewee, not the interpreter.

Managing Overlapping Turns in Police Interviews

It is commonplace for the two speakers in an interview or conversation to speak at the same time or have an interval of overlapped talk. The parties try to express their thoughts as they occur to them, or feel they have to respond to the other party there and then, rather than waiting for their turn. Situations like this present interpreters with additional challenges (Berk-Seligson, 1990), and, in the case of bilingual police interviews or courtroom discourse, make the task of transcribing and, later on, translating interviews a nightmare. Interpreters must be mindful of overlapped talk and manage the situation carefully as there may be claims later on that some crucial information was not interpreted at the time. Ignoring one of the parties, or explicitly allowing one of the parties to continue, may serve one party more than the other. Trying to wait to the end and then interpreting what each party said during the exchange would add to the cognitive load of the interpreter and would not be feasible to maintain over prolonged periods. The best course of action may be to stop interpreting and say to the parties that the interpreter is having difficulty following the exchange or conversation. Then it would be the responsibility of the parties to take action on the overlapped part by, for example, repeating the exchange one person at a time. In police interviews, the police officer is responsible for managing what is said, when it is said, and who says it.

Managing Deliberate Attempts to Undermine Communication

Just as in any other communicative events, the interviewee in a police interview, for whatever reason, may decide not to say anything (e.g., "no comment" interview), or may choose to give completely irrelevant answers, or remotely related responses. It is not uncommon for interpreters to find themselves having to deal with situations where a suspect or witness hysterically laughs at a question, screams, does not answer at all, or answers a question with a question, or provides a totally irrelevant statement in response to a question. These sorts of responses certainly add to the cognitive load of the interpreter as it is another aspect of the interaction that the interpreter has to deal with on top of the main task of transferring meaning between the parties. Interpreters in such situations should not feel obliged to "do something," such as prodding the suspect/witness, making suggestions, or giving advice about possible consequences of not answering the questions in order to orient the interview to a more productive outcome for the interviewing officer.

Sometimes a suspect/witness may claim that they do not understand what has been interpreted to him/her, and often this is regarded by other participants in the setting as a language issue or interpreting problem. The interpreter must refrain from attempting to reword or paraphrase the segment he/she just interpreted to make it more understandable for the suspect/witness. It is the role of the police officer to decide whether difficulty in communication is a deliberate attempt on the interviewee's part and then to decide what to do about it. Just as in monolingual settings when a police officer finds that the interviewee does not appear to understand a question just posed, the police officer would, more likely than not, reword or paraphrase the question and put it to the interviewee again. This should not be any different in a bilingual setting where the judgment call should be left to the police officer to make.

Dealing with Nonfluency and Paralinguistic Features

The term *nonfluency features* in language refer to such things as repetition (e.g., of something just said), hesitations (e.g., using fillers, such as uhms and ahs, slowing down and stretching words and sentences longer, using silence, etc.), and false starts (starting with one or a few words and suddenly stopping and saying something different). The interpreter must preserve the nonfluency features of the original speech as much as he/she can, as these features may be significant for the investigating police officers (Gonzales et al., 1991, p. 17). Interpreters tend to focus more on conveying the meaning and prioritize it over relaying the hesitations or false starts in the speech. False starts (where the speaker starts speaking, then suddenly stops and then says something different) can contain significant clues in police interviews as they reflect utterances people say without much thinking or planning.

Example:

Witness: "The two guys … (false start), the threat letter was placed in the letter box."

Interpreters should avoid omitting false starts, even if it is a small or incomplete utterance, such as the one in the example above. It is tempting to think that false starts are insignificant or irrelevant so the energy is better spent on going ahead to interpret the grammatically complete utterances that follow. However, false starts, such as "the two guys …," "my partner …," "the contract …" may contain information that may be significant for or of interest to the police officer and, therefore, should be reproduced in the other language. Omission of such aspects of a dialogue would be difficult to justify.

Another change of state token "Oh?" indicates that information is "new" to the receiver, which may encourage the speaker to continue to talk and give more information as they can see the receiver is interested, whereas expressions such as "yes" or "mm hm" or "okay" made by the receiver do not generally highlight the prior talk as "informative," thus discouraging the speaker from providing more information (Heritage, 1984, p. 307). As discussed earlier in Chapter 4 (Handling Interviewer's Rapport-Building Strategies), some of these emphatic markers may be a strategy used by the interviewing officer for rapport building purposes in an investigative interview. This is an aspect of a conversation and interview that should ideally be maintained by professional interpreters in order to minimize unjustified intervention.

The term *paralinguistic features* relates to nonspoken communication that does not involve words, e.g., body language, facial expressions, and prosodic elements, such as tone, intonation, and accent. Copying and recreating the speaker's body language, facial expression, and intonation in the other language by the interpreter is by no means an easy task. So, given the difficulty of conveying these paralinguistic features of a dialogue, should it be attempted at all? This is an area of contention and the authors are of the view that the interviewing police officer is able to pick up most of the paralinguistic features directly from the interviewee, and, therefore, most of the interpreter's cognitive capacity should be invested in the linguistic output, incorporating features, such as intonation or tone where appropriate and when possible.

Maintaining "Hedges"

Hedge is defined as "a particle, word, or phrase in a set; it says of that membership that it is partial, or true only in certain respects" (Brown & Levison, 1978, p. 150). Hedges are found to "leave the addressee the option of deciding how seriously to take what the speaker is saying" (Lakoff, 1975, p. 66). In legal contexts, speakers may use hedges to mitigate or soften the impact of the point they are making. They can be used to reduce criminal culpability in the legal setting. For example:

- I guess ...
- As I recall ...
- You might say ...
- Well ...

Hedges create the impression that the speaker is hesitant and, therefore, not as confident in the statement given. They weaken the certainty of an assertion. They are more likely to be used with damaging or unfavorable assertions, e.g., "I don't think I verbally abused her," but not with positive or favorable assertions, e.g., "I was always very polite." They, therefore, are significant and should not be overlooked by interpreters in their rendition into the target language (TL).

Strengthening/Clarifying Answers

Interpreters, knowingly or unknowingly, may add information to emphasize their interpreted utterances, as they are often evaluating their own interpreting as they go along and looking for better expressions. This leaves them exposed to scrutiny at later stages in the legal process, as they may find it difficult to justify their intervention.

Example (Strengthening):

PO: Did you hit him in the head?
Int: xx xxx x xx xx xxx x? (Did you hit him in the head?)
S/W: xx xxx. (No way).
Int: No, no way I would do such a thing.

Example (Clarifying)

PO: Who was first in?
Int: xx xx xxxx xx? (Who was first in?)
S/W: xxx xxx, xxx xxxx? (You mean, to the shop?)
Int: You mean, who broke into the shop first?

Hyperformality

Hyperformality refers to the interpreter expressing an utterance in a more formal discourse than the source utterance produced by the speaker. It also happens when there is a lack of ellipsis. In other words, the interpreter gives the complete form of the utterance instead of omitting the lexical items that are clear from the context. This is often done not deliberately on the interpreter's part, but still results in an unjustified intervention. U.S. linguistics professor Susan Berk-Seligson (2002) identifies hyperformality as one of the areas where significant interpreter errors occur. She finds that interpreters tend to interpret in hyperformal style, which changes the register of the source language (SL) and influences perceptions about the speaker by giving him/her an "enhanced image" (Berk-Seligson, 1989, p. 85). Hyperformality is characterized by (1) lack of ellipsis (syntactic omissions), (2) lack of commonly used contractions, and (3) lexical choices in a higher register (Berk-Seligson, 1990, p. 171). As hyperformal utterances tend to be wordy, Berk-Seligson's contention seems to conform to the research done by U.S. forensic linguist William O'Barr (1982), which proved that "narrative-like testimonies tend to be evaluated more positively than fragmented ones" (Berk-Seligson, 1989, p. 88).

Example (hyperformality):

PO: What did you do with the documents?
Int: xxx xx xx xxx xx xxxxxxx? (What did you do with the documents?)

S/W: xxx x xxx xxx xx xxx (Had a good look at the stuff.)
Int: I examined the documents thoroughly.

Example (hyperformality in English/Turkish):

Lawyer: Of what country are you a citizen?
Int: Hangi ülkenin vatandaşınız? (Of what country are you a citizen?)
S/W: Türkiye. (Turkey)
Int: I am a citizen of the Republic of Turkey.

The complete grammatical rendering by the interpreter as shown in the above two examples makes the utterances more formal and also may make the suspect/witness appear more "competent, intelligent, and trustworthy than the interpretation in a less formal register did" (Berk-Seligson, 1989, p. 87). As the authors have advocated so far, this sort of intervention effected by the interpreter may be problematic and hard to justify when and if it is called into question.

Managing Multicomponent Questions and Answers: "Chunking" Issues

Multicomponent questions, such as: "Did you go home after leaving the pub or did you stop elsewhere?" (Frankel, 1990, as cited in Heydon, 2005, p. 100) are generally not regarded as good interviewing techniques, and police officers are discouraged from asking multicomponent questions in their interviews with suspects/witnesses. This is simply because a "yes" or a "no" answer may mean a number of things, e.g., "Yes, I went home," "yes, I stopped somewhere else." In practice, however, such questions are not that uncommon in interviews and interpreters need to be aware of these structures as they can become more complicated in an interpreted interview. If the suspect/witness responds to one part of a multicomponent question without waiting for the other components to be interpreted, this needs to be indicated to the police officer. Otherwise, the police officer may assume that the answer relates to part of the question that is not intended by the interviewee. If an interpreter manages to reproduce the multicomponent question in the other language and the suspect/witness responds: "Yes," this then becomes the responsibility of the police officer to clarify, not the interpreter.

Suspects/witnesses also may construct an answer to a police question in which additional information is provided. The first component of the answer will often be a complete answer, but the suspect/witness may continue to provide information after a short pause. The interpreter needs to be aware of this when chunking. Early starts (as soon as the interpreter hears the answer to the question asked) may lead to a loss of information by prematurely interrupting the utterances of the suspect/witness.

Example:

PO: So wadcha do then?

S/W: w'I made meself another cup of coffee and I just thought about it. and I said what's going on this can't be right. Betty and I are getting on alright. I don't go anywhere near their house unless I phone. I ring her I say can I go and get this and that. She says yep, no worries.

(...)

I go to the shop there a couple aw every second day or third day and get milk bread and a few vegies and that I need and smokes. and we get on all right just as friends. (...)

(Heydon, 2005. p. 102)

All this information is provided following the police officer's question: "So wadcha do then?" After giving a direct answer: "made meself another cup of coffee," the suspect/witness continues with a monologue and provides information voluntarily. Interpreters generally tend to start interpreting after they hear the answer (or what they think is the answer) to the question asked. In the example above, this sort of early start would have discouraged the suspect/witness from continuing and providing further details and would be an unjustified intervention by the interpreter.

Managing Clarification

It is common that during an interview what is said and meant by the parties may not always be clear and may need clarification for the sake of accuracy. This is no different in a bilingual interview than a monolingual one. Consider the following example in a monolingual setting where the interviewing officer tries to clarify the people involved in the event:

PO: Just a second ago you said that he was well known in the area. Who were you referring to?

S/W: xx xxxx…(my boss).

In a bilingual setting, for example, in the Turkish language, the third person/object pronoun is indicated by the letter "o" for all singular persons and objects, whereas, in English, it is *she, he,* and *it*. If an interviewee starts a Turkish utterance with the pronoun "o," the interpreter would have to clarify who or what they were talking about first, unless it is obvious from the immediate context.

When interpreters seek clarification in video- or audio-recorded interviews, they should indicate this by announcing, e.g., "The interpreter needs to ask Mr. A to clarify."

Example from an interpreted-interview:

PO: What time did your uncle call you?

If this was to be interpreted to a Mandarin-speaking suspect, the interpreter would need to clarify whether it is the father's brother or the mother's brother and also whether the person that is referred to is younger or older than the suspect's parents, before they can come up with an equivalent in Mandarin. It is because the kinship system has not been lexicalized in the same way in all languages. Although, in this particular example, a briefing prior to the interview would have clarified issues such as this, initiating clarification is still quite often needed in bilingual interviews to confirm understanding or clear ambiguities. Generally, the main reason clarification requests need to be handled carefully is that it may appear to be a small conversation between the interpreter and one of the parties to the exclusion of the other party—a common area of concern in interpreted interviews. Before asking for clarification from the police officer, the interpreter should advise the interviewee that the interpreter needs to clarify a point with the police officer and then put it to the police officer, who can then clarify it for the interpretation to continue. The same principle applies when clarifications are needed for the statements made by the suspect/witness. These sorts of requests for clarification are justified, as they are needed to prevent a possible breakdown of communication or distortion of information that may affect the interview farther down the track.

The example above shows that what appears to be a simple utterance, such as "uncle" in English, may require a lengthy clarification process to convey it accurately into another language. The way the clarification is handled in a tape/video-recorded interview is as important as the clarification itself. The need for clarification must be justified, as in the above examples, and be explained to the other party. Otherwise, one of the parties will not know what is going on because the interpreter will appear to be having a conversation with the other party.

The issue of poor handling of clarifications is identified in two of the significant errors specified in the case of *Katsuno et al. v. Australia* (2006):

3. Arbitrarily asking his or her own questions of the defendants.
7. Long exchanges in Japanese with the defendants, with no participation by the investigator, and simple summarizations, often inaccurate, of what had transpired.

The following is an example of bad practice in clarifying an ambiguity:

PO: What did you do after you left the shop?
Int: xxx xxx xx xxxxx xxx xx? (What did you do after you left the shop?)
S/W: xxxx xx xxxx. (I walked to the club.)
Int: xxx xxx? (Which club?)
S/W: xxx xx (Fishing.)
Int: I walked to the fishing club.

In this example, an interpreter considers the answer ambiguous and initiates a clarification process, without advising the police officer. In future transcripts of the interview, only the police officer's question and the interpreter's interpreted segment into English would be included. The rest of the exchange would not appear.

In contrast, a good practice in clarifying a point can be as follows:

PO: You'll be charged with obtaining property by deception.
Int: (to the suspect) xxxx xxx xxx (I need to clarify something, and then to the interviewing officer) I am not sure if I heard you correctly, did you say: "You will be charged"?

This is a practical way of indicating to the suspect what the conversation that is about to take place between the interpreter and the police officer relates to, thus preventing any future claims that there were private conversations or even collusion between the interpreter and one of the other parties.

Sometimes, it may be best to let the parties sort it out through further questioning, as in the following lengthy exchange:

PO: Just before you said "us," what did you mean?

Int: xxxx xxxx xx xxxx "xxxx," xx xxx xxxx xx xxxx? (Just before you said "us," what did you mean?)

S/W: xxx xx? (Did I?)

Int: Did I?

PO: Yes. You said "us." Who else was there?

Int: xxx, xxx xxx "xx." xxx xx xxx xx xxx? (Yes. You said "us." Who else was there?)

S/W: xxxxxx. (Nobody.)

Int: Nobody.

PO: Why did you say "us" then?

Int: xxx xx xx xxxxx xxxx? (Why did you say "us" then?)

S/W: Uhm, xx xxx xx xxx x xx! (Uhm, I meant me and my dog!)

While this constitutes a lengthy clarification process, it minimizes intervention by the interpreter by allowing the parties to sort it out for themselves, as it would be in a normal monolingual interview.

Summary

This chapter illustrated some common nonlinguistic issues in interpreted police interviews that are applicable across a wide range of languages. In the previous chapter, we have worked through some common linguistic transfer issues, which tend to be the first, if not the only, aspect that comes to interpreting users' minds when assessing the quality of interpreting. We have explained that there are other challenges, such as interpersonal, intrapersonal, and environmental factors (Dean & Pollard, 2001) with which interpreters also have to deal. The principles we advocate above to manage these nonlinguistic issues in interpreted interviews are consistent with the recommendations made in the previous two chapters—interpreters should opt for a course of action that least interferes with the intentions or actions of the two parties for which they are interpreting. As the sheer presence of the interpreter in the bilingual police interview already creates a certain level of intervention (compared with a monolingual interview where the police interviewer and the suspect/witness do not need to communicate through a third party), the interpreter's performance can be assessed by whether their intervention is "justified" or "unjustified" when viewed from the standpoint of their professional role in the interview—in other words, helping both parties to communicate with each other.

6
CONCLUSION

Interpreting is managing the transfer of meaning between two different worlds, not just two different languages, as Sapir (1949) rightly observes. Whether interpreting is treated as a critical link in the form of a "conduit" or "pipe" linking two worlds and languages, or it is likened to a piece of gum stuck under the shoe (Morris, 1999), it has been around since the first contact between different tribes and civilizations (Piller & Takahashi, n.d.) and still happens every single day in current times.

As Laster and Taylor (1994, p. 136) highlight, "... access to an interpreter during police questioning is probably more significant than the right to an interpreter in court proceedings." There is an ever-growing need for highly qualified and specialized interpreters in this crucial initial stage of the criminal justice process.

This book has attempted to draw attention to the critical service provided by interpreters in interviews between police officers and suspects/witnesses. It has offered insight into this context both from an interpreting as well as from an investigative interviewing point of view.

One of the aims of the book is to link police investigative interview techniques and interpreting skills to allow for specialization of interpreters in this field, and to highlight some quality markers for interviewing officers to use when working with interpreters.

In all multilingual situations, the need for the accurate and impartial transmission of utterances between people or groups who do not have a language in common is imperative, not least when the transactions are carried out within the legal system. Because all of our social services, including the police forces, are under time and funding constraints, access to impartial, accurate, well-trained interpreters can only be of benefit. The reduction in stress levels alone would be invaluable, and the contribution to good, clear communication within a community, immeasurable. Good quality interpreting, including a high standard of professional practice will not only help to avoid miscarriages of justice in some cases, but also will contribute to making sure that all parties involved come properly through the legal process.

We hope the discussions in this book have contributed to a greater comprehension of the role of interpreting in investigative interviewing, and its development as a specialist area of interpreting practice. Toward fostering this understanding, this book has offered a summary of the special features of interpreting in police interview settings, and indicated some of the specialist skills and considerations that are relevant to such a setting. It identifies a number of critical areas where the actions of interpreters may knowingly or unknowingly interfere in the police interview and may impact on the success of the interview or quality of interpreting. We hope that greater and more widespread recognition of this field of interpreting will prompt more research in the area, conferences on the topic, and opportunities for cooperation and collaboration between police agencies and the interpreting profession globally.

References

Allimant, A., Martinez, B., & Wong, E. (2006). Changes and challenges in the therapeutic relationship when using an interpreter. In *Lighting the path: Reflections on counselling, young women and sexual assault* (pp. 151–165). Brisbane: Zig Zag Young Women's Resource Centre.

Anderson, R. B. W. (1976/2002). Perspectives on the role of interpreter. In F. Pöchhacker & M. Shlesinger (Eds.), *The interpreting studies reader*. London: Routledge.

Angelelli, C. V. (2004). *Revisiting the interpreter's role. A study of conference, court and medical interpreters in Canada, Mexico and the United States*. Amsterdam/Philadelphia: John Benjamins.

Atkinson, J. M. (1992). Displaying neutrality: Formal aspects of informal court proceedings. In P. Drew & J. Heritage (Eds.), *Talk at work* (pp. 199–211). Cambridge: Cambridge University Press.

AUSTLII 2013(a). *Crimes Act 1958–Sect 464D*. Retrieved May 1, 2013, from: http://www.austlii.edu.au/au/legis/vic/consol_act/ca195882/s464d.html

AUSTLII 2013(b). *Evidence Act 1995–Sect 30*. Retrieved May 1, 2013, from: http://www.austlii.edu.au/au/legis/nsw/consol_act/ea199580/s30.html

AUSTLII 2013(c). *Interpretation Act 1984–Sect 18*. Retrieved May 1 2013, from: http://www.austlii.edu.au/au/legis/wa/consol_act/ia1984191/s18.html

Baker, M. (1992). *In other words: A course book on translation*. Abingdon/New York: Routledge.

BBC *News*. (2012). The collapses at Snaresbrook court after interpreter error. Retrieved from:http://www.bbc.co.uk/news/uk-england-london-17709440

Benmaman, V. (1992). Legal interpreting: An emerging profession. *The Modern Language Journal*, 76(4), 445–453.

Benmaman, V. (1997). Legal interpreting by any other name is still legal interpreting. In S. E. Carr, R. P. Roberts, A. Dufour, & D. Steyn (Eds.), *The critical link: Interpreters in the community* (pp. 179–190). Amsterdam/Philadelphia: John Benjamins.

Berk-Seligson, S. (1989). The role of register in the bilingual courtroom: Evaluative reactions to interpreted testimony. *International Journal of the Sociology of Language, 79*, 79–91.

Berk-Seligson, S. (1990). *The bilingual courtroom: Court interpreters in the judicial process.* Chicago: The University of Chicago Press.

Berk-Seligson, S. (2000). Interpreting for the police: Issues in pre-trial phases of the judicial process. *Forensic Linguistics, 7*(2), 213–238.

Berk-Seligson, S. (2002). The Miranda warnings and linguistic coercion: The role of footing in the interrogation of a limited English-speaking murder suspect. In J. Cotterill (Ed.), *Language in the legal process* (pp. 127–143). Hampshire/New York: Palgrave Macmillan.

Berk-Seligson, S. (2009). *Coerced confessions: The discourse of bilingual police interrogations.* New York/Berlin: Mouton de Gruyter.

Bittner, E. (1970). *Functions of police in modern society.* Washington, D.C.: U.S. Government Printing Office.

Blake, B. J. (1981). *Australian aboriginal languages.* Sydney: Angus & Robertson.

Brown, P., & Levison, S. (1978). Politeness phenomena. In E. N. Goody (Ed.), *Questions and politeness: Strategies in social interaction* (pp. 56–289). New York: Cambridge University.

Buckley, J. (2006). The Reid technique of interviewing and interrogation. In T. Williamson (Ed.), *Investigative interviewing: Rights, research, regulation* (pp. 190–206). Devon, U.K.: Willan Publishing.

Cai, X-h, & Fang, F-q. (2003). *Assessment of interpreting quality and effect. Foreign languages and Teaching Press, 3*, 41–45.

Carrabine, E., Cox, P., Lee, M., Plummer, K., & South, N. (2013). *Criminology: A sociological introduction.* Retrieved from: http://rmit.eblib.com.au.ezproxy.lib.rmit.edu.au/patron/FullRecord.aspx?p=401830

CHAG. (2004). *Lost in translation: A discussion paper on interpreting issues in health care settings in Queensland Multicultural Development Association.* Rockhampton, QLD: Cannon Hill Action Group (CHAG).

Chisholm, R. (2007). *Understanding law.* Sydney: LexisNexis.

Code C Detention, Treatment and Questioning of Persons by Police Officers, Police and Criminal Evidence Act 1984 (1984).

Cotterill, J. (2002). *Language in the legal process.* Hampshire/New York: Palgrave Macmillan.

Coulthard, M. (2002). Whose voice is it? Invented and concealed dialogue in written records of verbal evidence produced by the police. In J. Cotterill (Ed.), *Language in the legal process* (pp. 19–34). Hampshire/New York: Palgrave Macmillan.

Coulthard, M., & Johnson, A. (2007). *An introduction to forensic linguistics: Language in evidence.* New York: Routledge.

Danet, B. (1980). Language in the legal process. *Law and Society Review, 14*, 445–564.

Danks, J., Shreve, G. M., Fountain, S. B., & McBeath, M. K. (Eds.). (1997). *Cognitive processes in translation and interpreting*. Thousand Oaks, CA: Sage Publications.

Dean, R. K., & Pollard, R. Q. (2001). The application of demand-control theory to sign language interpreting: Implications for stress and interpreter training. *Journal of Deaf Studies and Deaf Education, 6*(1), 1–14.

de Jongh, E. M. (2012). Court interpreting and due process. In *From the classroom to the courtroom: A guide to interpreting in the U.S. justice system*. Amsterdam/Philadelphia: John Benjamins.

Dillinger, M. (1994). Comprehension during interpreting: What do interpreters know that bilinguals don't? In B. Lambert, & S. Moser-Mercer (Ed.), *Bridging the gap: Empirical studies in simultaneous interpretation* (pp. 155–189). Amsterdam/Philadelphia: John Benjamins.

Evans, G. & Webb, M. (1993). High profile—but not that high profile: Interviewing of young persons. In E. Shepherd (Ed.), *Aspects of police interviewing*. Leicester, U.K.: British Psychological Society.

Fairclough, N. (1989). *Language and power*. London: Longman.

Fisher, R., & Castano, N. (2008). Cognitive interview. In B. Cutler (Ed.), *Encyclopedia of psychology and law* (pp. 95–100). Thousand Oaks, CA: Sage Publications.

Frankel, R. (1990). Talking in interviews: A dispreference for patient-initiated questions in physician-patient encounters. In G. Psathas (Ed.), *Interaction competence* (pp. 231–262). Washington, D.C: University Press of America.

Frishberg, N. (1990). *Interpreting: An introduction* (Rev. ed.). Alexandria, VA: RID Press.

Gaio vs. The Queen. (1961). *Melbourne University Law Review, 3*(2), 237–240. Retrieved from http://www.austlii.edu.au/au/journals/MelbULawRw/1961/26.html

Geiselman, R. E., & Fisher, R. P. (1985). Interviewing victims and witnesses of crime. *National Institute of Justice/Research in Brief,* December, 1–4.

Gerver, D. (1971). *Aspects of simultaneous interpretation and human information processing*. Oxford, U.K.: Oxford University.

Gibbons, J. (1990). Applied linguistics in court. *Applied Linguistics, 11*(3), 229–237.

Gibbons, J. (2007). *Forensic linguistics: An introduction to language in the justice system* (2nd ed.). Oxford, U.K.: Blackwell.

Gibson, J. (2006, March 13). Plenty of warnings for 'bloody' ad ban. *The Age*. Retrieved from: http://www.theage.com.au/news/national/plenty-of-warnings-for-bloody-ad-ban/2006/03/13/1142098394237.html

Gile, D. (1995). *Basic concepts and models for interpreter and translator training*. Amsterdam/Philadelphia: John Benjamins.

Gile, D. (2009). *Basic concepts and models for interpreters and translator training* (revised edition). Amsterdam/Philadelphia: John Benjamins.

Goffman, E. (1981). *Forms of talk*. Philadelphia: University of Pennsylvania Press.

González, R. D., Vásquez, V. F., & Mikkelson, H. (1991). *Fundamentals of court interpretation: Theory, policy and practice*. Durham, NC: Carolina Academic Press.

González, R. D., Vásquez, V. F., & Mikkelson, H. (2012). *Fundamentals of court interpretation: Theory, police and practice* (2nd ed.). Durham, NC: Carolina Academic Press.

Granhag, P. A., Strömwall, L. A., & Hartwig, M. (2007). The SUE-technique: The way to interview to detect deception. *Forensic Update*, 88, 25–29.

Greatbatch, D. (1988). A turn-taking system for British news interviews. *Language in Society, 17*(03), 401–430.

Gudjonsson, G. H. (1992a). *The psychology of interrogations, confessions and testimony*. Chichester, U.K.: John Wiley & Sons.

Gudjonsson, G. H. (1992b). The psychology of false confessions and ways to improve the system. *Expert Evidence: The International Digest of Human Behaviour Science and Law, 1*, 49–53.

Gudjonsson, G. H. (1999). Police interviewing and disputed confession. In A. Memon & R. Bull (Eds.), *The psychology of interviewing* (pp. 327–341). Chichester, U.K.: John Wiley & Sons.

Gudjonsson, G. H. (2003). *The psychology of interrogations, confessions and testimony*. Chichester, U.K.: John Wiley & Sons.

Gudjonsson, G. H., & Pearse, J. (2011). Suspect interviews and false confessions. *Current Directions in Psychological Science, 20*(1), 33–37. doi: 10.1177/0963721410396824

Hale, S. (2004). *The discourse of court interpreting: Discourse practices of the law, the witness and the interpreter*. Amsterdam/Philadelphia: John Benjamins.

Hale, S. (2007). *Community interpreting*. Hampshire/New York: Palgrave Macmillan.

Hale, S. B., & Gibbons, J. (1999). Varying realities patterned changes in the interpreter's representation of courtroom and external realities. *Applied Linguistics, 20*(2), 203–220.

Hartwig, M., Granhag, P. A., Strömwall, L. A., & Vrij, A. (2005). Detecting deception via strategic disclosure of evidence. *Law and Human Behaviour*, 29(4), 469–484. doi: 10.1007/s10979-005-5521-x.

Hartwig, M., Granhag, P. A., Strömwall, L. A., & Kronkvist, O. (2006). Strategic use of evidence during police interviews: When training to detect deception works. *Law and Human Behavior*, 30(5), 603–619. doi: 10.1007/s10979-006-9053-9

Haworth, K. (2006). The dynamics of power and resistance in police interview discourse. *Discourse and Society, 17*, 739–759.

Heritage, J. (1984). A change-of-state token and aspects of its sequential placement. In J. M. Atkinson & J. Heritage (Eds.), *Structures of social action: Studies in conversation analysis* (pp. 299–345). Cambridge: Cambridge University Press.

Heritage, J. (1985). Analysing news interviews: Aspects of the production of talk for an overhearing audience. In T. A. V. Dijk (Ed.), *Handbook of discourse analysis* (Vol. 3, pp. 95–117). London: Academic Press.

Heydon, G. (2005). *The language of police interviewing: A critical analysis*. New York: Palgrave Macmillan.

Holliday, R. E., Brainerd, C. J., Reyna, V. F., & Humphries, J. E. (2009). The Cognitive Interview: Research and Practice across the Lifespan In R. Bull, T. Valentine, & T. Williamson (Eds.), *Handbook of psychology of investigative interviewing: current developments and future directions*. Chichester, West Sussex: Wiley-Blackwell.

Jacobsen, B. (2011). Translation disparity leads to aborted trial. *The Age*. Retrieved from: http://www.theage.com.au/national/translation-disparity-leads-to-aborted-trial-20111107-1n44x.html#ixzz1d4Ex8Voz

Jakobson, R. (1959). *On linguistic aspects of translation*. Retrieved May 1, 2012 from: http://www.stanford.edu/~eckert/PDF/jakobson.pdf

Jalbert, M. (1998). *Travailler avec un interprète en consultation psychiatrique*. *P.R.I.S.M.E. 8* (3), 94–111.

Kahane, E. (2000). *Thoughts on the quality of interpretation*. Retrieved May 1, 2013 from:http://aiic.net/page/197/thoughts-on-the-quality-of-interpretation/lang/1

Kaji, H. (1999). Controlled languages for machine translation: State of the art. *MT Summit VII* (September), 37–39.

Kamasinski v. Austria (1989). European Court of Human Rights (UCHR). Retrieved 1 March, 2013, from http://echr.ketsc.com/doc/9783.82-en-19891219/view/

Kassin, S. M. (1997). The psychology of confession evidence. *American Psychologist, 52*(3), 221–233.

Kassin, S. M., & McNall, K. (1991). Police interrogations and confessions: Communicating promises and threats by pragmatic implications. *Law and Human Behavior, 15*(3), 233–251. doi: 10.1007/BF01061711

Katan, D. (1999). *Translating cultures: an introduction for translators, interpreters and mediators*. Manchester: St. Jerome.

Katsuno et al. v. Australia (2006). United Nations Human Rights Committee. Retrieved 1 February, 2013, from http://www.ag.gov.au/RightsAndProtections/HumanRights/DisabilityStandards/Documents/KatsunoOrsvAustralia-Viewsof31102006.doc

Krouglov, A. (1999). Police interpreting: politeness and sociocultural context. *The Translator, 5*(2), 285–302.

Lai, M., & Mulayim, S. (2013). Interpreter linguistic intervention in the strategies employed by police in investigative interviews. *Police Practice and Research: An International Journal*, 15(4), DOI: 10.1080/15614263.2013.809929

Lakoff, R. (1975a). *Language and woman's place*. New York: Harper & Row.

Lakoff, R. (1975b). The Miranda warnings and linguistic coercion: The role of footing in the interrogation of a limited-English-speaking murder suspect. In J. Cotterill (Ed.), *Language in the legal process* (pp. 127–143). Hampshire/New York: Palgrave Macmillan.

Laster, K. (1990). Legal interpreters: Conduits to social justice? *Journal of Intercultural Studies, 11*, 16–32.

Laster, K., & Taylor, V. L. (1994). *Interpreters and the legal system*. Sydney: The Federation Press.

Leanza, Y. (2005). Roles of community interpreters in pediatrics as seen by interpreters, physicians and researchers. *Interpreting, 7(2)*, 167–192.

Leanza, Y. (2007). Roles of community interpreters in pediatrics as seen by interpreters, physicians and researchers. In F. Pöchhacker & M. Shlesinger (Eds.), *Healthcare interpreting: Discourse and interaction* (pp. 11–34). Amsterdam/Philadelphia: John Benjamins.

Lederer, M. (2003). *Translation: The interpretive model.* Manchester and Northampton, MA: St. Jerome.

Lee, J. (2009). When linguistic and cultural differences are not disclosed in court interpreting. *Multilingual, 28*, 379–401. doi: 10.1515/mult.2009.017

Leung, E. S. M. (2003). Rights to be heard and rights to be Interpreted. *Babel, 49*(4), 289–301.

Levinson, S. C. (1992). Activity types and language. In P. Drew & J. Heritage (Eds.), *Talk at work: Interaction in institutional settings* (pp. 66–100). New York: Cambridge University Press.

Lord, V. B., & Cowan, A. D. (2011). *Interviewing in criminal justice: Victims, witnesses, clients, and suspects.* Sudbury, MA: Jones and Bartlett Publishers.

Magliano, J. (2014). Reasonable doubt: Demonstrating how subtle features of language might influence juror decisions [2 April]. Retrieved from http://www.psychologytoday.com/blog/the-wide-wide-world-psychology/ 201402/reasonable-doubt

McGurk, B., Carr, J., & McGurk, D. (1993). *Investigative interviewing courses for police officers: An evaluation.* London: Home Office. (H. Office, Trans.)

Mikkelson, H. (1999). *Verbatim interpretation: An oxymoron.* Retrieved May 1, 2013, from: http://www.acebo.com/papers/verbatim.htm

Miller, K. R. (2001). Access to sign language interpreters in the criminal justice system. *American Annals of the Deaf, 146(4)*.

Milne, R. & Bull, R. (1999). *Investigative interviewing: Psychology and practice.* Chichester, U.K.: John Wiley & Sons.

Morris, R. (1999). The gum syndrome: Predicaments in court interpreting. *International Journal of Speech, Language and the Law, 6*(1), 6–29.

Morris, R. (2008). Missing stitches. An overview of judicial attitudes to interlingual interpreting in the criminal justice systems of Canada and Israel. *Interpreting, 10*(1), 34–64.

Morris, R. (2010). Images of the court interpreter. *Translation and Interpreting Studies, 5*(1), 20–40.

Munday, J. (2008). *Introducing translation studies: Theories and applications.* Abingdon, U.K./New York: Routledge.

Nakane, I. (2009). The myth of an 'invisible mediator:' An Australian case study of English–Japanese police interpreting. *Journal of Multidisciplinary International Studies, 6*(1), 1–16.

National Crime and Operations Faculty. (2003). *Association of chief police officers investigative interview strategy: Training curriculum.* Bramshill: Centrex/ National Crime and Operations Faculty.

O'Barr, W. M. (1982). *Linguistic evidence: Language, power and strategy in the courtroom*. New York/London: Academic Press.

O'Connor, J., & Seymour, J. (1990). *Introducing NLP neuro linguistic programming*. London: Mandala.

Order in the Court: the lighter side of the law. From the verbatim columns of *Bar news*. (1988). Melbourne: Lothian.

Ord, B., Shaw, G., & Green, T. (2011). *Investigative interviewing explained*. Chatswood, N.S.W: LexisNexis Butterworths

Ozolins, U. (2009). Social workers, The law and interpreters. In P. Swain & S. Rice (Eds.), *In the shadow of the law: The legal context of social work practice* (pp. 20–35). Sydney: The Federation Press.

PACE. (1984). Police and Criminal Evidence Act 1984 Section 13, Code C: Detention, Treatment and Questioning of Persons. Retrieved 1 March, 2013, from https://www.gov.uk/government/uploads/system/uploads/attachment_data/file/306657/2013_PACE_Code_C.pdf

Paltridge, B. (2006). *Discourse analysis*. London/New York: Continuum.

Peräkylä, A., & D. Silverman (1991). Owning experience: Describing the experience of other persons. *Text*, *11*(3), 441–480.

Perez, I. A. & Wilson, C. W. L. (2007). Interpreter-mediated police interviews. In C. Wadensjö, B. E. Dimitrova, & A.-L. Nilsson (Eds.). *The Critical link 4: Professionalisation of interpreting in the community*. Selected papers from the 4th International Conference on Interpreting in Legal, Health and Social Service Settings, (pp. 79–93), Stockholm, Sweden, May 20–23, 2004. Amsterdam/Philadelphia: John Benjamins.

Piller, I., & Takahashi, K. (n.d.). Language, migration and human rights. Retrieved May 1, 2013, from http://www.languageonthemove.com/downloads/PDF/piller_takahashi_in%20press_human%20rights.pdf

Pöchhacker, F. (2007). Critical linking up: Kinship and convergence in interpreting studies. In C. Wadensjo, B. E. Dimitrova, & N. A.-L. (Eds.), *The Critical Link 4* (pp. 11–26). Amsterdam/Philadelphia: John Benjamins.

Quah, C. K. (2006). *Translation and technology*. Hampshire/New York: Palgrave MacMillan.

Roberts, R. P. (2002). Community interpreting: A profession in search of its identity. In E. Hung (Ed.), *Teaching translation and interpreting 4: Building bridges* (pp. 157–175). Amsterdam/Philadelphia: John Benjamins.

Roberts-Smith, L. (2009). Forensic Interpreting: Trial and Error. In S. B. Hale, U. Ozolins & L. Stern (Eds.), *Critical link 5: Quality in interpreting - A shared responsibility* (pp. 13–36). Amsterdam and Philadelphia: John Benjamins.

Rogers, C. R. (1942). *Counselling and psychotherapy*. Boston: Houghton Mifflin.

Roy, C. (2000). *Interpreting as a discourse process*. Oxford/New York: Oxford University Press.

Russell, S. (2002). 'Three's a crowd:' Shifting dynamics in the interpreted interview. In J. Cotterill (Ed.), *Language in the legal process* (pp. 111–126). Hampshire/New York: Palgrave Macmillan.

Sacks, H., Schegloff, E. A., & Jefferson, G. (1974). A simplest systematics for the organisation of turn-taking for conversation, *Language, 50*(4i), 696–735.

Sapir, E. (1956). *Culture, language and personality: Selected essays.* Berkeley: University of California Press.

Schollum, M. (2005). *Investigative interviewing: The literature.* Wellington: New Zealand Police.

Schön, D. A. (1983). *The Reflective practioner.* New York: Basic Books.

Shepherd, E. (1988). Developing interview skills. In P. Southgate (Ed.), *New directions in police training.* London: HMSO.

Shepherd, E. (2007). *Investigative interviewing: The conversation management approach.* Oxford/New York: Oxford University Press.

Silvester, J. (2010). Police learn the art of gentler persuasion. *The Age.* Retrieved from: http://www.theage.com.au/victoria/police-learn-the-art-of-gen-tler-persuasion-20100906-14y02.html

Swanson, L., C. R. Chamelin, & N. C. Territo. (2002). *Criminal investigation.* Burr Ridge, IL: McGraw-Hill Higher Education.

Tipton, R. (2010). On trust: Relationships of trust in interpreter-mediated social work encounters. In M. O. Baker & M. A. C. Pérez, (Eds.), *Text and context: Essays on translation & interpreting in honour of Ian Mason.* (pp. 188–208). Manchester, U.K./Kinderhook, NY: St. Jerome Publishing.

Turner, B., & Ozolins, U. (2007). The standards of linguistic competence in English and LOTE among NAATI accredited interpreters and transla-tors. Retrieved from RMIT University website: http://mams.rmit.edu. au/6vzzapomxpxez.pdf

United Nations International Covenant on Civil and Political Rights. (1966). Retrieved October 10, 2010, from: http://www2.ohchr.org/english/law/ccpr.htm

United Nations International Covenant on Civil and Political Rights. (2006). Communication no. 1154/2003 (Vol. 2013). Geneva: UN CCPR.

U.S. Department of Justice. Executive Order 13166. Retrieved May 1, 2012, from U.S. Department of Justice: http://www.justice.gov/crt/about/cor/13166.php

Vessel, D. (1998). Conducting successful interrogations. *FBI Law Enforcement Bulletin, 67*(10), 1–6.

Viaggio, S. (2000). Aptitude and simultaneous interpretation: A proposal for a testing methodology based on paraphrase. In G. V. Garzone & M. Viezzi (Eds.), *Interpreting in the 21st century: Challenges and opportunities* (pp. 231–246). Amsterdam/Philadelphia: John Benjamins.

Vredeveldt, A. (2011). *The benefits of eye-closure on eyewitness memory* (Doctoral dissertation). University of York, U.K. Retrieved from: http://annelies. vredeveldt.com/wp-content/uploads/2012/04/PhD-thesis-Annelies-Vredeveldt.pdf

Vredeveldt, A., Baddeley, A. D., & Hitch, G. J. (2013). The effectiveness of eye-closure in repeated interviews. *Legal and Criminological Psychology.* doi: 10.1111/lcrp.12013

Vredeveldt, A., Hitch, G. J., & Baddeley, A. D. (2011). Eye-closure helps mem-ory by reducing cognitive load and enhancing visualisation. *Memory & Cognition, 39,* 1253–1263.

Wadensjö, C. (1998). *Interpreting as interaction*. Harlow: Longman.

Walkley, J. (1987). *Police interrogation. A handbook for investigators*. London: A Police Review Publication.

Wells, W. (1991). *An introduction to the law of evidence*. Adelaide, SA: A. B. Caudell.

Westermeyer, J. (1990). Working with an interpreter in psychiatric assessment and treatment. *Journal of Nervous and Mental Disease, 178*(12), 745–749.

Index

Advances in
POLICE THEORY and PRACTICE

Presenting volumes that focus on the nexus between research and practice, this series is geared toward those practitioners and academics seeking to implement the latest innovations in policing from across the world. This series draws from an international community of experts who examine who the police are, what they do, and how they maintain order, administer laws, and serve their communities.

Books in this Series:

Honor-Based Violence
Policing and Prevention
Karl Anton Roberts, Gerry Campbell, and Glen Lloyd
Catalog no. K15429, November 2013
227 pp., ISBN: 978-1-4665-5665-2

Security Governance, Policing, and Local Capacity
Clifford D. Shearing and Jan Froestad
Catalog no. 90143, December 2012
257 pp., ISBN: 978-1-4200-9014-7

Policing and the Mentally Ill
International Perspectives
Edited by
Duncan Chappell
Catalog no. K13821, May 2013
381 pp., ISBN: 978-1-4398-8116-3

Policing White-Collar Crime
Characteristics of White-Collar Criminals
Petter Gottschalk
Catalog no. K20530, December 2013
339 pp., ISBN: 978-1-4665-9177-6

Financial Crimes
A Threat to Global Security
Edited by
Maximillian Edelbacher, Peter C. Kratcoski, and Michael Theil
Catalog no. K13172, June 2012
488 pp., ISBN: 978-1-4398-6922-2

The Crime Numbers Game
Management by Manipulation
John A. Eterno and Eli B. Silverman
Catalog no. K10516, January 2012
282 pp., ISBN: 978-1-4398-1031-6

Police Integrity Management in Australia
Global Lessons for Combating Police Misconduct
Louise Porter and Tim Prenzler
Catalog no. K14262, April 2012
296 pp., ISBN: 978-1-4398-9598-6

Most titles also available as eBook

Series Editor

Dr. Dilip K. Das is president of the International Police Executive Symposium, IPES, www.IPES.info. He is also a human rights consultant to the United Nations. Dr. Das has over 40 years of experience in police practice, research, writing, and education. He is founding editor-in-chief of *Police Practice and Research: An International Journal*.

Advances in POLICE THEORY and PRACTICE

This **Advances in Police Theory and Practice** series encourages the contribution of works coauthored by police practitioners and researchers. Proposals for contributions to the series may be submitted to the series editor Dr. Das, at **dilipkd@aol.com** or directly to:

Carolyn Spence, Senior Editor
CRC Press / Taylor & Francis Group
carolyn.spence@taylorandfrancis.com

Published

Police Corruption
Preventing Misconduct and Maintaining Integrity
Tim Prenzler
Catalog no. 77961
March 2009

Community Policing
International Patterns and Comparative Perspectives
Edited by
Dominique Wisler and Ihekwoaba D. Onwudiwe
Catalog no. 93584
June 2009

Community Policing and Peacekeeping
Edited by
Peter Grabosky
Catalog no. K10012
June 2009

Security in Post-Conflict Africa
The Role of Nonstate Policing
Bruce Baker
Catalog no. 9193X
August 2009

Policing Organized Crime
Intelligence Strategy Implementation
Petter Gottschalk
Catalog no. K10504
August 2009

The New Khaki
The Evolving Nature of Policing in India
Arvind Verma
Catalog no. K10722
December 2010

Mission-Based Policing
John P. Crank, Rebecca K. Murray, Dawn M. Irlbeck, and Mark T. Sundermeier
Catalog no. K12291
August 2011

Police Reform in China
Kam C. Wong
Catalog no. K11036
October 2011

The International Trafficking of Human Organs
A Multidisciplinary Perspective
Edited by
Leonard Territo and Rande Matteson
Catalog no. K13082
October 2011

Los Angeles Police Department Meltdown
The Fall of the Professional-Reform Model of Policing
James Lasley
Catalog no. K14343
August 2012

Police Performance Appraisals
A Comparative Perspective
Serdar Kenan Gul and Paul O'Connell
Catalog no. K11803
September 2012

Forthcoming Titles!

Police Investigative Interviews and Interpreting
Context, Challenges, and Strategies
Sedat Mulayim, Miranda Lai, and Caroline Norma
Catalog no. K23394
October 2014

Crime Linkage
Theory, Research, and Practice
Jessica Woodhams and Craig Bennell
Catalog no. K14634
August 2014

Women in Policing
An International Perspective
Venessa Garcia
Catalog no. K16281
June 2015

Democratic Policing
Darren Palmer
Catalog no. K20353
June 2014

Islamic Women in Policing
A Contradiction in Terms?
Tonita Murray
Catalog no. K10720
March 2015

Female Criminals
An Examination and Interpretation of Female Offending
Venessa Garcia
Catalog no. K16301
June 2014

Policing in Hong Kong
History and Reform
Kam C. Wong
Catalog no. K14267
December 2014

Civilian Oversight of Police
Advancing Accountability in Law Enforcement
Edited by
Tim Prenzler and Garth den Heyer
Catalog no. K22986
September 2014

Policing Terrorism
Research Studies into Police Counter-terrorism Investigations
David Lowe
Catalog no. K22506
January 2015

Police Leadership in the 21st Century
Responding to the Challenges
Jenny Fleming and Eugene Mclaughlin
Catalog no. K12766
September 2015

Corruption Fraud, Organized Crime, and the Shadow Economy
Edited by
Maximillian Edelbacher, Peter C. Kratcoski, and Bojan Dobovsek

Collaborative Policing
Peter C. Kratcoski and Maximillian Edelbacher

Visit us online at
www.crcpress.com

A Call for Authors
Advances in Police Theory and Practice

AIMS AND SCOPE:

This cutting-edge series is designed to promote publication of books on contemporary advances in police theory and practice. We are especially interested in volumes that focus on the nexus between research and practice, with the end goal of disseminating innovations in policing. We will consider collections of expert contributions as well as individually authored works. Books in this series will be marketed internationally to both academic and professional audiences. This series also seeks to —

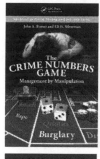

The CRIME NUMBERS GAME
Management by Manipulation
John A. Eterno and Eli B. Silverman

Police Reform in China
Kam C. Wong

- Bridge the gap in knowledge about advances in theory and practice regarding who the police are, what they do, and how they maintain order, administer laws, and serve their communities
- Improve cooperation between those who are active in the field and those who are involved in academic research so as to facilitate the application of innovative advances in theory and practice

Mission-Based Policing
John P. Crank
Rebecca K. Murray
Dawn M. Irlbeck
Mark T. Sundermeier

The International Trafficking of Human Organs
A Multidisciplinary Perspective
Leonard Territo and Rande Matteson

The series especially encourages the contribution of works coauthored by police practitioners and researchers. We are also interested in works comparing policing approaches and methods globally, examining such areas as the policing of transitional states, democratic policing, policing and minorities, preventive policing, investigation, patrolling and response, terrorism, organized crime and drug enforcement. In fact, every aspect of policing, public safety, and security, as well as public order is relevant for the series. Manuscripts should be between 300 and 600 printed pages. If you have a proposal for an original work or for a contributed volume, please be in touch.

Series Editor
Dilip Das, Ph.D., Ph: 802-598-3680
E-mail: dilipkd@aol.com

Dr. Das is a professor of criminal justice and Human Rights Consultant to the United Nations. He is a former chief of police, and founding president of the International Police Executive Symposium, IPES, www.ipes.info. He is also founding editor-in-chief of *Police Practice and Research: An International Journal* (PPR), (Routledge/Taylor & Francis), www.tandf.co.uk/journals. In addition to editing the *World Police Encyclopedia* (Taylor & Francis, 2006), Dr. Das has published numerous books and articles during his many years of involvement in police practice, research, writing, and education.

Proposals for the series may be submitted to the series editor or directly to —
Carolyn Spence
Senior Editor • CRC Press / Taylor & Francis Group
561-317-9574 • 561-997-7249 (fax)
carolyn.spence@taylorandfrancis.com • www.crcpress.com
6000 Broken Sound Parkway NW, Suite 300, Boca Raton, FL 33487